DISNEYLAND
HONG KONG 2024

Hong Kong, Asia's Wonderland! A Travel Guide to Make your First Trip Easy.

Ellen P. Peterside

TABLE OF CONTENTS

A Brief Overview: Hong Kong Disneyland

The Walt Disney Company entered the Chinese theme park industry with its first venture, Hong Kong Disneyland. Between the ground-breaking ceremony in January 2003 and the park's debut in September 2005, the theme park was constructed in a very short amount of time. The primary goal of the theme park was to boost tourism in Hong Kong, particularly in the wake of the 2003 SARS pandemic that severely damaged the local economy. The Walt Disney Company and the Government of Hong Kong jointly own the park.

The theme park is situated in a gorgeous tropical setting that is unmatched by any other Disney park. It is conveniently located in relation to Hong Kong. From the city center, it is approximately $200HK for a 2-minute taxi ride, $100HK for a 10-minute ride, or $100HK for a 10-minute ride from Hong Kong International Airport. Alternatively, you can take the widely used MTR train system for between $15 and $20HK, which drops you off right at the resort.

Main Land Shanghai Disneyland, China's larger Disney theme park complex, is a radically distinct facility. While Shanghai Disneyland has been an enormous success, Hong Kong Disneyland is often considered as Disney's least successful resort.

With 6.7 million visitors in 2018, Hong Kong Disneyland is the second-least popular Disney theme park worldwide, behind Walt Disney Studios Park in Paris. Away from busy times such as Christmas

Travel Advice

18 Insider Suggestions For The Most Amazing Visit to Disneyland in Hong Kong

At some point in their lives, everyone hopes to travel to the happiest spot on earth. Disney World
There is plenty to adore about this enchanted location. You may go on exhilarating rides that will make your heart race, meet your favorite Disney character, and take in the nighttime fireworks display.

These 18 suggestions will ensure that your trip is one you won't soon forget, from how to navigate the crazy lines to the best halal food around!

1. Use paperless e-tickets to bypass the lines!
Disneyland may be a fun location, but battling the crowds to get a ticket? Not in that way. And spend even more time on your favorite rides and attractions, get your entry tickets on Klook and escape the never-ending lines at the ticket booths!
In addition to receiving rapid confirmation of your purchase, all you need to do to enter the park is scan the barcode on your mobile e-ticket! Totally hassle-free and devoid of crowds, allowing you to fully enjoy your enchanted journey.

- HHWT # Advice: Simply swap the e-ticket at the AutoMagic Tickets machine if you would prefer to keep the paper ticket!

- The tickets available on Klook are open-dated, so even if your travel plans aren't set in stone, you can visit Hong Kong Disneyland whenever you choose. You can select between a 1- or 2-day ticket.

- P.S. A 2-day ticket would be ideal if you're going with young children so you can take your time touring the park without wearing them out!

2. **Verify the opening hours beforehand and get there early.**

Please take note that we do not mean to arrive 10 minutes early. Even an hour before the park opens, expect to see lines of people waiting in line!

Additionally, because the park opened 15 minutes ahead of schedule the last time we visited, we advise you to confirm the opening timings in advance. The best course of action would be to visit the official website before heading to the park.

The MTR in Hong Kong makes it simple to travel to Disneyland, as the train makes handy stops directly at the park station.

- HHWT # Advice: We advise purchasing a MTR pass if you want to use public transit throughout your multi-day visit in Hong Kong! Purchase a MTR travel pass on Klook to have unrestricted access to the MTR system for three days. The best method to get to the city is via air, and the pass includes a single or return trip on the Airport Express! In order to have the freedom to move around without your bags, don't forget to check in at the Airport Express station 90 minutes to a full day prior to your scheduled flight.

- HHWT # As an alternative, you can choose to leave your bags at Hong Kong Disneyland itself as they offer luggage valet services!

3. Get a Fastpass so you can skip the queue.

Everybody enjoys visiting Disneyland, therefore it makes sense that every ride will have an unbelievably lengthy queue and much longer wait times, particularly during busy times. So, reduce the amount of time you have to wait by getting a Fastpass!

- The Fastpass system gives you a fixed time to enter an attraction, which helps you cut down on wait times at several attractions. Go to the Fastpass ticketing machines by the attraction's entrance and scan your entry ticket under the reader to obtain your Fastpass. The attraction must be visited again within the window of time specified on your Fastpass ticket.

Only these attractions are eligible for Fastpass+:

- Hyperspace Mountain in The Many Adventures of Winnie the Pooh

- Please be aware that the Fastpass is limited, so reserve yours in advance to avoid disappointment!

4. **Purchase goods by 1pm to receive 10% off.**
A trip to Disneyland would not be complete without indulging in the cutest character goods. Additionally, you can get 10% off merchandise if you buy it before 1pm! That makes it even more motivation to get that enormous plush toy of Winnie the Pooh that you've had your eye on.
Although there are many tiny stores in Hong Kong Disneyland that offer items (such Andy's Toy Box and Pooh Corner, to mention a couple), the Emporium unquestionably boasts the largest selection! You'll need an additional suitcase for your haul of goodies, which includes limited-edition mementos, keychains, themed clothing, and even a cap with personalized Mickey Mouse ears.

5. Savor delicious halal-certified cuisine.
Upon returning from an enjoyable day out, are you hungry, fellow Muslims? The fact that Hong Kong Disneyland is the only one in the world with cuisine certified halal makes it really fantastic.
Refuel at the Explorer's Club Restaurant or Tahitian Terrace Restaurant, which provide a variety of dishes including Korean, Japanese, and even Indonesian.

6. Take advantage of fantastic meal discounts with Klook's meal voucher!
With Klook's Hong Kong Disneyland meal voucher, you may save money on your lunch in addition to savoring the delectable buffet! Both of the park's halal-certified restaurants accept this coupon.
To redeem this promotion, just like any other paperless Klook transaction, you just need to present your e-voucher while placing your order and making your payment.

7. Offer up your prayers in the allocated prayer space.

Finding a suitable location to pray while visiting Hong Kong Disneyland is not a concern! There is a special prayer room in the park reserved for Muslim guests, and it is situated directly next to the Explorer's Club Restaurant.

8. Download the FREE Hong Kong Disneyland app and get a pocket WiFi.

Are you curious about the wait time for a feature that's located on the opposite side of the park? To find out, download the Hong Kong Disneyland app for free! In addition to monitoring the wait times for different attractions, you may also discover which locations and attractions are closed on that particular day, the time of the parade, a virtual park map, and more.

The app will also notify you of alternate weather plans in the event of inclement weather. Get the useful software right away—it's accessible on iOS and Android!

While the virtual park map indicates the various locations with free WiFi, it can be a little patchy in certain areas. Invest in a small WiFi device so you can remain connected while traveling! You may easily arrange for a pick-up from the Hong Kong Airport if you make reservations on Klook.

9. **Gather complimentary Disney stickers from the cast members.**

Get stickers from the cast to create the perfect collection of stickers with a character theme! These extremely sought-after stickers are carried by almost every cast member in the park, including housekeeping employees and those working in the businesses. Asking is all that is required.

- You'll have to wander around the park and speak with different cast members if you want a variety of stickers because they're available in different places of the park (for example, Tomorrowland has Star Wars stickers, while Fantasyland has Beauty and the Beast stickers).

10. **Take home personalized items**

You may even personalize your own products at Hong Kong Disneyland! Visit Centre Street Boutique's personalization center to take advantage of their calligraphy, engraving, floral, and embroidered services.

11. **Visit the Festival of the Lion King to relive your childhood.**

There's no need to introduce The Lion King if you grew up in the 1980s or 90s! Like a short musical, the tale of everyone's beloved cartoon lion is condensed into only thirty minutes. Acrobatic acts, fire dancers, and flashing strobe lights accompany the giant floats featuring your favorite characters, Simba, Timon, and Pumbaa.

12. **Ignore the meet and greets and go directly to the sights.**

Though you'll have plenty of chances to say hello to your fave Disney characters throughout the day, you'll be tempted to do so as soon as you walk through the main doors. Be the first in queue and head straight for the rides. You will see Mickey and Minnie later on during the floating parade, so don't worry.

- Maybe you could take a picture with the rest of Mickey's friends instead of standing in line to take a picture with him at Main Street, which is close to the park's entrance. If Mickey and Minnie are busy entertaining other visitors, Goofy, Pluto, Donald, and Daisy are anxious to say hello.

- Alternatively, decide to visit Fantasyland's Sleeping Beauty Castle to meet Cinderella, Aurora, Snow White, Rapunzel, and Belle, the five stunning princesses! This meeting won't be one of you yawning your way through.Additionally, visit your robotic companion, BB-8, in the Tomorrowland Command Post!

- Get your tickets on Klook and start organizing your trip before you head out to see these princesses or BB-8! If a single day isn't long enough to meet all of these endearing personalities, you may choose for a 2-day ticket, which will ensure that the fun doesn't end at dusk.

13. **Begin your investigation at the farthest end.**

Make a thorough route plan and go directly to the locations that are farthest from Main Street. You'll have the advantage of avoiding the crowd even if other fans might be star struck, lining up for a picture with Mickey or excitedly standing in queue for the first ride they see.

14. Skip the shows to cut down on wait times
Popular showtimes have shorter snake-line lines for the hottest rides. Can you live without seeing the parade performances? The queue for the Big Grizzly Mountain Runaway Mine Cars at Grizzly Gulch is considerably less crowded than it usually is.

15. You can get stunning photos from places other than PhotoPass Picture locations!
Take wanderlust photos at other sites rather than looking for PhotoPass Picture locations. On board the Hong Kong Disneyland Railroad train, record your own memories! Either in Fantasyland or Main Street, hop aboard the locomotive, then relax and take in the aerial view of your childhood palace. You won't want to miss it—it will really be a spectacular experience.

16. **Spend the night in hotels near Disneyland**

There's no better way to cap off the day than with a comfortable stay fit for a true Disney enthusiast like you. at this manner, lovely dreams at the happiest spot on Earth are assured. The following day, have breakfast at the Enchanted Garden with Mickey, Minnie, and Pluto while lounging in the specially constructed suites—there are never any lines!

- HHWT # Advice: Disney's Hollywood Hotel (Chef Mickey and Studio Lounge) and Hong Kong Disneyland Hotel (Walt's Cafe and room service) all offer halal-certified meals upon request.

- Depending on the kind of hotel room reserved, guests at any of the three hotels are entitled to a minimum of one Priority Admissions Pass for park attractions. Priority passes to three attractions are given to guests staying in the Sea View room at Disney Explorers Lodge, while permits to four attractions are given to those staying in the Kingdom Club room at Hong Kong Disneyland Hotel!

- Make sure you reserve a seat for the Lion King musical celebration if you plan to spend the night in a Sea View accommodation at Disney Explorers Lodge or the Hong Kong Disneyland Hotel.

- All lodging categories include passes to the Iron Man Experience, It's a Small World, Big Grizzly Mountain Runaway Mine Cars, and Mystic Manor attractions. The attractions Slinky Dog Spin, The Many Adventures of Winnie the Pooh, and Toy Soldier Parachute Drop are available to those staying in Sea View or above room type priority passes.

17. **Take part in joyful events with your Disney family.**

During Halloween, go trick-or-treating; during Easter, look for chocolate bunnies. Whether or not you are celebrating, the festive décor will put you in the mood for a joyous occasion! Take in the vibrant environment and indulge in a little fun as you see how holidays such as Halloween, Easter, and

Christmas are celebrated in a land where fantastical events are always in store.

18. **Bring along a few useful essentials.**

It might seem apparent, but you're sure to overlook a few things when your enthusiasm and adrenaline kick in. Fortunately, our purpose is to remind you. When you're done applying, slide the sunscreen into your bag and don't forget the bug repellent! To battle a humid day when traveling in the summer, bring a portable fan. Regardless matter the weather—sunny or rainy—put that little umbrella in your clutch because even Mickey is prepared for a downpour.

A THREE-DAY PACKAGE TOUR OF HONG KONG DISNEYLAND FOR FAMILIES WITH CHILDREN

A World of Magic and Fun for Your Kids at Various Ages

The biggest theme park in Hong Kong, Hong Kong Disneyland, is a great place to take kids when they are visiting the city. You and your children are sure to have a great time at Disneyland in Hong Kong with a plethora of Disney characters to meet, rides to enjoy, a Lion King show, the Fantasy Parade, and fireworks. Explore seven themed areas, including Fantasyland, Toy Story Land, and Adventureland. These areas feature all of the must-see rides, including Space Mountain, Mad Hatter Tea Cups, and It's a Small World, in addition to several that are exclusive to Hong Kong Disneyland.

In addition to fantastic exploration in Hong Kong Disneyland, here is included some kid-friendly activities in this tour of Hong Kong, such as learning new things at museums (Science, History, or Space Museums), taking the Peak Tram up to Victoria Peak, taking an interesting Star Ferry across Victoria Harbour, or having fun at the playground with neighborhood kids.I have no doubt that, when you and your children go at a proper leisure pace, you would "LOVE Hong Kong"!

Alternate Plan: If you've been to Disneyland previously, you and your children can spend the second day seeing Ocean Park (where you can see dolphins) and Aberdeen Fishing Village. Alternatively, you can inform us the ages and interests of your children before making any decisions, and we will be happy to provide you and your family with a personalized Hong Kong trip!

DAY 1 ARRIVAL IN HONG KONG

Recommended activities for families with children: Avenue of Stars - Temple Street Night Market

Hello! Welcome to Hong Kong, Asia's World City, to unpack your dreams.
Upon arrival, a local guide will be ready to meet you at the airport, train station, harbor or metro station. From there, you will then be taken to your hotel for where you'll settle in. The rest of your time will be spent exploring this modern metropolis.
Recommended activities for families with children (find yours):

Take a leisurely walk on the Boulevard of the Stars at night.
Enjoy stunning views of Victoria Harbor and Hong Kong Island with its many skyscrapers.
Enjoy the Symphony of Lights every night at 8pm.

Next, take a stroll through Temple Street Night Market, Hong Kong's liveliest night market.
From souvenirs to small trinkets, clothes, shoes and bags, you and your kids will love them.

You can find a variety of beautifully designed products to browse and, if you wish, taste some delicious food as well.
At the end of the tour, you will be returned to your hotel.

DAY 2 HONG KONG DISNEYLAND

Explore Hong Kong Disneyland for a full day with 7 theme parks.

After breakfast, transfer to Hong Kong Disneyland, the first Disney resort in China.
Inspired by the dream of fairy tales, entered the magic kingdom and later entered with seven, mysterious, mysterious, toys, Roman, Will, Will and Maine, United States.
-Beauty, Emotion and Disney characters.

I like the heat with American Main Street.

If you want to get your imagination from your imagination, we know a special opportunity to live the Disney character.

Karus and Carus walk on a horse and climbed into the classic Disney story, passing through the classic Disney story, wiping the story of Daml Disci and surprising Disney at the 3D concert.

Go to a part of the toy and receive a toy in this pure blue barrel, remove toys with toys with toys, tense jumps, Disney Pixar Toy Toy Story Story and remove the big queues and food around them.

Reservoir; With my mysterious thought, this is an excellent 3D gene to 3D 3D.

Grizzly Gulch, Travicon, line and lines are left like garbage and leave the train in the speed field.

In the middle of Star Wars, you go through freedom and "free contact" and steel war, you have a careful meeting with the marsh superhero man and you get a high level along the planet.

If you have a passion for adventure and emotion, go to an interesting and negative river to high adventures and visit the tall adventures in the peasant.

HONG KONG DAY 3 AND DEPARTURE FROM HONG KONG

Victoria Peak - Star Ferry - Middle Road Playground - Hong Kong Science Museum

Finish with breakfast, your tour guide and driver will pick you up from your hotel and to the agreed destination.

First, take the kids on the legendary Peak Tram, one of the oldest cable cars and in operation for over 130 years, the fastest and most beautiful way to reach Victoria Peak, the highest point on Hong Kong Island (552 of meters).
Oh gosh. vehicle.

Climb aboard the Sky Terrace 428 observation deck and enjoy incredible 360-degree panoramic views of the vibrant city, from the beautiful skyline and Victoria Harbor to tranquil green landscapes. If you want, you can walk around and take beautiful photos.

After descending from Victoria Peak, the family travels to Central Pier for a comfortable Star Ferry ride across Victoria Harbour.

The Star Ferry was named one of National Geographic's "50 Places to Visit in a Lifetime".

Take a 10-minute ride on the green and white ferry and take great photos of Hong Kong's beautiful skyline from the boat.
After arriving at Tsim Sha Tsui Pier, take a stroll along the Tsim Sha Tsui Promenade, which offers spectacular views from Victoria Harbor to Hong Kong Island.
Then enjoy some fun and relaxation at the Middle Road Children's Playground.
With swings and slides for all ages, this airfield is a community utopia for children of all ethnicities.

The last stop of the day is a visit to the Hong Kong Science Museum.
The action-packed three-story pavilion at Hong Kong's liveliest museum is a great place for youngsters from babies to teenagers to learn something new.

Browse nearly 500 exhibits in the permanent exhibition space and see the world's largest

22-meter twin-tower power machine. (Note: The Hong Kong History Museum is opposite the Science Museum. You can choose to visit either the Science Museum or the History Museum.

This wonderful historical museum brings the city's history to life in colorful ways.
Your kids will enjoy Hong Kong history exhibits that beautifully recreate local traditions, including Chinese weddings and real fishermen.

The exhibition also takes you on a fascinating journey through the history of shaping the city and its culture, as well as the history of the region's development from its beginnings through British rule and unification with China in 1997.)

Chapter 1

PLANNING YOUR TRAVEL

It can be difficult to plan a trip to Hong Kong Disneyland. You need to consider things like lodging, meals, tickets to the parks, spending money, and transportation. By taking the actions listed below, this section should help you become ready. The ensuing chapters of this guide expand upon each of these steps.

Choose your mode of transportation: will you be arriving at the resort by train, taxi, or airplane? To ensure that your days are planned appropriately, find out when you will arrive at the resort and depart if you are taking public transport.

Make a decision about staying on- or off-site. Would you rather have the ease of being close to the magic? Or would you rather remain somewhere else?

Examine the official park map at https://www.hongkongdisneyland.com/maps/ . Select the shows and attractions you want to see by combining the information in this book with the map. Mark or jot down the ones you wish to visit on your map. To get the most out of your visit, you must be aware of the general locations of the park's attractions. Although you don't have to memorize the map, consulting it beforehand will help you make the most of your time when you get there.

The theme park adjusts its opening hours based on how busy it will be; the more visitors anticipated, the longer the park stays open. Park opening hours vary greatly. The most recent hours can be found https://www.hongkongdisneyland.com/calendars/day/ on the Hong Kong Disneyland website.

You can get a Tinies Guide by clicking on any date, which provides you with information on the parade and performance schedule, character locations and times, and other important details to know ahead of time. Unlike most other theme parks, Hong Kong Disneyland is open 365 days a year, therefore it does not set aside a specific time of year to close and conduct maintenance. Rather, throughout the year, the theme park temporarily closes its rides, shows, attractions, and park portions for renovations. To minimize the impact on visitors, this is typically done once a year for each attraction, preferably during slower times of the year.

A few months in advance, renovations are announced. Make sure to review the renovation schedule found on the calendar on https://www.hongkongdisneyland.com.

Go through this guide from cover to cover, take a screen grab of important pages, print them off, and carry it around on your phone, tablet, or e-reader.

British visitors are in luck because Hong Kong plugs are the same as those back home, but if you are traveling from outside the city, make sure to pack plug adapters (and maybe power converters)!
Ensure that you obtain your Hong Kong dollars ahead of time. Don't depend on purchasing cash at the airport. We advise using a credit or debit card with an 8% currency conversion rate, or obtaining a prepaid currency card that you can top off. Having cash on hand is always convenient.

Hong Kong: Be Aware Before Traveling

While going to Hong Kong and Hong Kong Disneyland is an exhilarating experience, many people find it intimidating, especially Westerners who may not have traveled to Asia before. You may travel to Hong Kong with ease if you can only understand English because, up until 1997, the city was governed by the British, making it feel quite westernized.

PASSPORTS

Important: Before you schedule your trip, make sure to confirm that the information below is still accurate about visas. Regulations and rules are subject to change, so please take this section with a grain of salt. The key is to plan!

Hong Kong is incredibly welcoming to tourists, as citizens of almost 170 different nations are not required to have a visa in order to enter. Visas are not needed for citizens of the US, Europe, Australia, Canada, or New Zealand, and they can stay for up to 90 days (180 days for UK citizens). Even if your stay is only for seven days in some nations, you'll still have plenty of time to tour Disneyland and Hong Kong.

Those who do not qualify for visa-free travel must apply to their local Chinese embassy or consulate in order to obtain a Hong Kong visa. Processing this normally takes four weeks. https://www.chinadiscovery.com/chinese-visa/hong-kong-visa.html.

CURRENCY AND PAYMENTS

Chinese use the Hong Kong dollar. The symbol for this is HK$, and it is frequently shortened to HKD. Since 1983, the US dollar has determined the value of the Hong Kong dollar, hence the ratio between the two has always been fixed.

As of this writing: -AU$1 = HK$4.93 -CA -NZ$1 = HK$4.67$1 represents HK$5.54 - US$1 = HK$7.75 - €1EUR = $HK8.43 -£1GBP = HK$9.7O

Visitors visiting Hong Kong have access to a wide range of payment options. In addition to cash, credit and debit cards (mostly Visa, Mastercard, and occasionally American Express) are also commonly accepted in major cities. The Octopus public transport card is frequently recognised at convenience stores and fast-food restaurants in Hong Kong, however it is not accepted at Disneyland. It is used on the MTR system of the city.

Many places also accept mobile wallets like Apple Pay and Android Pay, however we've had a lot of problems using them with international bank accounts. As a tourist, you won't require these for cash, nevertheless. Often debit and credit card are used by all and everywhere.

All of Hong Kong Disneyland's shops and restaurants that offer Table Service and Quick

Service accept cash as well as credit/debit cards. While some theme park vendors accept credit cards, the majority only accept cash for minor foods like ice cream.

Hong Kong Disneyland takes cash in RMB (mainland Chinese Yuan) in addition to Hong Kong Dollars. But throughout the rest of Hong Kong, this isn't the case.
The majority of credit and debit cards in Hong Kong are swipe-only and do not require PINs. ATMs and card terminals may occasionally need a PIN; however, PINs issued in Hong Kong typically consist of six digitals, as opposed to the four digitals used in the USA and Europe. Try your PIN normally in this scenario; if it doesn't work, you'll need to put two zeros before it.

TIPPING
Tipping is typically anticipated in restaurants, hotels, and taxis, while it is not required.
A hotel porter who has carried your stuff up to your room would feel insulted if you gave them less than HK$10–20, yet the doorman who opens the taxi for you will accept HK$10. Additionally, you ought to give something for the maid who cleaned your

room; if you were well-cared for during your five- or six-night stay, HK$100 is reasonable.

A 10% service charge is often automatically added to your bill (though not always), but it's not certain that the money goes towards paying the wait staff. If you feel that you have received good service, you could want to add an extra 5–10% to this.

It is appropriate to round up the fee to the nearest Hong Kong dollar on short taxi rides. For a lengthier ride, tip five Hong Kong dollars.

Safety of Food and Water

The cuisine in Hong Kong is highly regarded and often made with fresh ingredients. There should be no stomach issues because even the dai pai dongs at the side of the road follow strict sanitary standards. You should probably stay away from oysters and other shellfish if your stomach is more sensitive than average.

Since nothing is wasted, several meat slices that could be thrown away elsewhere are easily accessible here. There's no shortage of chances for those who enjoy sampling different cuisines!

Ask whether you are sensitive to MSG as some of the less expensive restaurants use it in their food.

Those who are allergic to peanuts should check before placing an order because peanut oil may also be used.

Tap water is safe to drink unless your building has really outdated plumbing. However, bottled water is usually provided by your hotel and can be purchased at all supermarkets and convenience stores for a reasonable price. Although the tap water at the hotels and the theme park is safe to drink, visitors staying on-site at Hong Kong Disneyland are given many huge bottles of water each day.

LANGUAGES

Languages: The dialect of Cantonese Cantonese is the Chinese dialect that is spoken there. Additionally, this is said in the Languages: The Dialect of Cantonese Cantonese is the Chinese dialect that is spoken there. Situated approximately 70 miles north, Guangzhou, a prominent metropolis in Southern China, as well as other areas of the nearby province of Guangdong, also speak this language. Mandarin is the official language of China, and it is extremely distinct.

Although speakers of different dialects of Chinese may not be able to understand one another when speaking, everyone can comprehend the language when it is written down, whether it be using traditional or simplified characters.

Mainlanders have recently moved in large numbers. You are likely to hear Mandarin spoken because Mandarin speakers have been relocating to Hong Kong and mainland Chinese tourism has increased dramatically since the Chinese economy has expanded.

In addition, it is the most widely spoken language in the world and the popular second language at the many worldwide English-medium schools.

If you have an excellent ear for languages and would like to learn more, there are many Cantonese phrase books available. The locals will be amazed.

Is English A Common Language?
Fortunately, a sizable portion of Hongkongers speak some English, however this isn't necessarily the case in all areas of the New Territories. English is commonly spoken and understood in hotels, stores, and restaurants. It's also well understood throughout Hong Kong Disneyland, where everyone is fluent in the language. Uber can be a better

transportation choice if you have issues with taxi drivers.

Street signs and place names still bear strong British influences, and it is quite uncommon to come across written signs or public information that is not printed in Chinese characters with an English translation.

CLIMATE

Climate There are seasonal differences in the subtropical climate of Hong Kong. It experiences hot, muggy summers and chilly winters. As low as 8 °C (46 °F) can be reached throughout the winter.

Autumn brings warmth, sunshine, and dry weather; spring through summer brings heat, humidity, and rain.

May through September is when it gets unbearably hot, with high humidity and temperatures reaching up to 34 °C (93 °F). January is the driest month and May is the wettest. Rainfall totals for the year average 2638.3 mm (103.9 inches).

Although Hong Kong is a popular travel destination all year round, October and November often have the best weather. At this time, the humidity decreases and the days frequently get warmer. July and August are the least agreeable months, while September is frequently excessively humid as well.

Both typhoons and intense rainstorms are common in Hong Kong. For typhoons and heavy rain, the government has developed sophisticated warning systems. The Hong Kong Observatory issues numbered warning signals that are displayed in government buildings along with advice that are appropriate based on how close the typhoon's center or eye is. Typhoon is derived from the Cantonese term taifung, which means strong wind.
If there is a typhoon in the area, local media—such as radio, television, and newspapers—also update the public on its progress, and the Observatory regularly releases weather reports.

ELECTRICAL OUTLETS

Electrical Outlets: Similar to the UK, Ireland, Singapore, and United Arab Emirates, Hong Kong utilizes 220-240-volt power with three-pin square-ended plugs.
Convenience stores and hotel housekeeping departments both sell adapters.

Wi-Fi and facilities for making tea and coffee are standard in all but the most budget hotels.

Electric shavers can be used with most bathrooms' 110-volt or 220-volt two-point outlets. If there is anything you have forgotten, it is probably easily obtained locally, so don't worry.

Time and Hours of Daylight

The coordinates of Hong Kong are 22.4° North and 114.11° East. There are no long, light evenings here, and the amount of daylight hours varies just slightly from 11 in midwinter to 13.5 in summertime.

Given that it is located in Coordinated Universal Time zone +8, it is eight hours ahead of London in the winter and seven hours ahead in the summer. There isn't a daylight saving programme in place.

Cell phones, WiFi roaming, and Internet access.

If your home SIM card is enabled for roaming, your first choice for using your phone in Hong Kong is to utilise it for that purpose. But this comes at a price: nft"pn pynrhitanf — rHprlr XAritb vniir

CELL PHONES, WIFI ROAMING, AND INTERNET ACCESS

If your home SIM card is enabled for roaming, your first choice for using your phone in Hong Kong is to use it for that purpose. But the price for this is typically very high; inquire about pricing with your supplier; some charge very high rates, while others offer this service for a nominal daily, monthly, or even free of charge.

This is the easiest method because it requires no action on your part (except from turning on roaming on your phone). It simply functions; you don't need to change SIM cards and you keep your phone number.

SIP Card

Picking up a SIM card intended for international travel at the airport is preferable to purchasing a local one, which can be confusing. You will be able to utilise data with this SIM card when visiting Hong Kong. The price is really reasonable; 8 days of unlimited data would run you about £6, US$7, €7, or HK$55. Numerous further services are offered.

We advise examining Klook and contrasting the options to see which one best suits your needs. This website is a great place to get tickets and entertainment in Asia all in one place. You can buy the aforementioned SIM card at bit.ly/hksim.

Join up at this exclusive link to receive an exclusive HK$40 off your first booking: bit.ly/klookinvite.

E-Sim

In case you possess a contemporary smartphone that is compatible with this feature and you are more tech-savvy, we strongly advise utilizing an E-SIM. This is an additional virtual SIM card for your phone. To receive calls and messages, you can still use your regular SIM card and phone number, but you can use a virtual SIM card to use data. There is no need to order a card and then pick it up in person when you arrive—all you have to do is pay for your E-sim and then scan a QR code on your phone to activate it. We suggest checking out Airalo at www.bit.ly/gotoairalo. Plans range, with HKMobile offering 1GB for US$3.5, 3GB for US$7, and 5GB for US$10.50. As an alternative, Hong Kong Unicorn charges US$9 for eight days of unlimited data.

In April 2020, the following devices were listed as compatible with eSIM: iPhone 11, iPhone 11 Pro, iPhone 11 Pro Max, iPhone XS, iPhone XS Max, iPhone XR, iPhone SE2, Samsung Galaxy S20, Samsung Galaxy S20+, Samsung Galaxy S20 Ultra, Samsung Galaxy Z Flip, Nuu Mobile X5, Google

Pixel 3 &c3 XL, Google Pixel 3a &c 3a XL, Google Pixel 4 &:4 XL, Lenovo Yoga 630, HP Spectre Folio, iPad Air (3rd Generation), iPad Pro (3rd Generation), iPad Mini (5th Generation), Gemini PDA, Motorola Razr 2019 and Samsung Galaxy Fold.

Wi-Fi Lease
Additionally, Wi-Fi hotspot rental businesses like Uroaming are available at airports. Additionally, this is available for reservation on Klook at bit.ly/hkwifiroam for HK$ 18 per day per device.

Chapter 2

TRANSPORTATION

HOW TO TRAVEL TO DISNEYLAND IN HONG KONG

Mickey Mouse-shaped windows may be found at Hong Kong Disneyland's Disney Resort Line. The Mickey windows on the Disney Resort Line MTR train are a hit with everyone.

MTR From the heart of Hong Kong: The MTR makes it simple and affordable to travel to Hong Kong Disneyland. Ride the Tung Chung MTR line to Sunny Bay station (since they originate in Central, all trains on this line run in the same direction from Central). Change to the Disneyland Resort Line at Sunny Bay. The ride takes about twenty minutes and is rather easy.

You may reach the Disneyland Resort Line by using any of the other MTR lines that travel throughout Hong Kong to Sunny Bay. Because every train car has a map and English signage, the MTR is a simple underground system to navigate. The trains also use English to "speak." They're also spotless, most likely because you're not meant to eat or drink on them.

From Hong Kong International Airport: If there is no traffic, it takes approximately 15 minutes to reach Hong Kong Disneyland, despite the airport being located on Lantau Island. Make sure you get a blue taxi from Lantau. Kowloon, Central, and a few other areas of Hong Kong are served by red taxis.

Hotel Resort Shuttles

Disney lodging Between the three hotels and the Disneyland Resort Public Transport Interchange (PTI), guests can take the complimentary shuttle buses operated by Hong Kong Disneyland Resort. The PTI and Hong Kong Disneyland Park are only a short stroll away.

Via Bus

You can ride local and cross-border buses to and from Hong Kong Disneyland Resort.

Hong Kong Disneyland Resort is served by franchised bus lines that are provided every day by Long Win Bus, Citybus, and New Lantao Bus. Locate the bus schedule and route.

To get to the Hong Kong Disneyland Resort, travellers arriving via the Hong Kong-Zhuhai-Macau Bridge have two options: the Cross Border Bus or the Shuttle Bus. In about ten minutes, the Shuttle Bus route connects the Resort to the Hong Kong Port of the Bridge. Every day, a cross-border bus route crosses the bridge to connect Zhuhai, Macau, with Hong Kong Disneyland Resort.

Every day, a cross-border bus route connects Hong Kong Disneyland Resort with mainland China. See more information

By Car
By Car The Hong Kong Disneyland Resort welcomes cars, coaches, and motorcycles.

Use maps and simple directions to plan your route as you drive to Hong Kong Disneyland.

Motorbikes, buses, and vehicles can all park in Hong Kong Disneyland Park.

By Taxi: Avoid taking the taxi from Central if you don't have to because traffic in Hong Kong can be extremely difficult. On the other hand, I once took a taxi from the Hong Kong Disneyland Hotel to

Central Hong Kong around midday on a weekday, and it went well and wasn't too expensive.

Hong Kong Disneyland Resort is accessible to and from three taxi services. The color-coded taxi service districts are as follows: Taxis in cities (red) and the New Territories (green), Taxis in Lantau (blue).
The Disneyland Public Transport Interchange is where taxis drop off and pick up guests at Hong Kong Disneyland Resort (PTI).

From MTR
Get on the Disneyland Resort Line at Sunny Bay Station to take use of the handy Mass Transit Railway (MTR).
From early in the morning until late at night, trains departing from Sunny Bay Station and travelling to Hong Kong Disneyland Resort and back run every few minutes.
Go to the MTR website for the most recent information on train schedules.
The following MTR stations are only a 30-minute trip from Hong Kong Disneyland Resort:
Sunny Bay Station and Tsing Yi Station are the transfer stations for the MTR at Hong Kong International Airport.

With the Express Rail Link

West Kowloon in Hong Kong is connected to the Hong Kong/Shenzhen border via the 26-kilometer Hong Kong Section of the Guangzhou-Shenzhen-Hong Kong Express Rail Link. The MTR makes it easy to get from the West Kowloon Station to Hong Kong Disneyland Resort.

With the Guangzhou-Shenzhen Hong Kong Express Rail Link connecting the city to China's national express rail grid, the Hong Kong Disneyland Resort is now easier to get there than before. No matter what location they are from, visitors to Hong Kong Disneyland can take use of a number of practical transit alternatives after they arrive at the West Kowloon Station.

by Kowloon Station on the Mass Transit Railway (MTR)

When you get to West Kowloon Station, you can ride the MTR to Hong Kong Disneyland.

To go to the Hong Kong Disneyland Magic Gateway in the Arrivals Hall, turn right after the turnstiles in the Customs section.

Take the footbridge to Elements, a sizable shopping centre complex in Kowloon, and pay attention to the signage.

Proceed right through Elements and keep following the signs to "Kowloon Station."

When you get to Kowloon MTR Station, take the train heading towards Tung Chung by following the orange signage pointing to the Tung Chung Line.

Get off at Sunny Bay MTR Station and board the Disneyland Resort Line train on the platform across from it.

Once you get out of the station at the Hong Kong Disneyland Resort MTR Station, head towards the park or the hotel shuttles.

OCTOPUS CARD

The Octopus card will make your life much easier if you wish to move around Hong Kong with ease. It may be used on buses and other public transport, including the MTR. Moreover, department stores, supermarkets, convenience stores, retailers, booksellers, movie theatres, taxis, and other establishments accept the Octopus card for payments.

Octopus cards are available for purchase by visitors at KLOOK, MTR stations, and the Airport Express Customer Service Centre. With HKD 50 preloaded, it is priced at HKD 95. For HKD 222 (about USD 28.35), our affiliate partner KLOOK is also offering the Octopus Card - HKD 150 Preloaded + Hong Kong 4G SIM Card (8 days).

Chapter 3

PARK TICKETS

Hong Kong Disneyland Resort will increase ticket prices and introduce a new day pass tier for peak times, such as the Christmas season, which started on September 20, 2023.

Hong Kong Disneyland Resort had decided to alter its ticket pricing structure, with effect from September 20, 2023. One of the noteworthy changes is the increase in ticket costs, which is meant to guarantee the continuous delivery of outstanding experiences and services. Furthermore, a brand-new day pass tier will be unveiled especially for the most popular times of year, like the joyous Christmas season. The park's dedication to improving the whole visitor experience and meeting the rising demand during peak hours is reflected in these changes.

Purchasing tickets for Hong Kong Disneyland through a reliable affiliate like KLOOK is the fastest and most straightforward option.

Adult tickets for Hong Kong Disneyland in 2023 will cost:

- The official price of a one-day ticket is HKD 639; the KLOOK discounted price is HKD 590, or roughly USD 78.39.

- The official price for a two-day ticket is HKD 904; the KLOOK discounted price starts at HKD 768, or roughly USD 110.10.

- 2023 Children's (3–11) Hong Kong Disneyland ticket prices:

- The official price for a one-day ticket is HKD 475; the KLOOK discounted price is HKD 572, or roughly USD 59.65.

- The official price for a two-day ticket is HKD 679; the KLOOK discounted price is HKD 629, or roughly USD 83.55.

- Tickets for Hong Kong Disneyland for seniors (65 and over) in 2023:

- The official price of a one-day ticket is HKD 100; the KLOOK discount price is HKD 100, or roughly USD 13.29.

- Two-day ticket: HKD 170 is the official starting price; HKD 768 (about USD 22.59) is the KLOOK discount price.

- Please take note that Disney Premier Access and entry tickets are not sold together at Hong Kong Disneyland. Disney Premier Access is an additional purchase that must be made individually.

Reserve a Park

Similar to Disneyland in Anaheim, entry requires both a valid ticket and a reservation in advance. Ninety days prior to their visit, guests have the option to make a reservation.

After completing the transaction, if you bought your tickets from a third party, such as the affiliate KLOOK, you will need to check your email for the ticket number. Next, you will need to click on the link to the official Hong Kong Disneyland website and make a reservation in order to access the park.

DPA PREMIER ACCESS

Free FastPass is no longer available at Hong Kong Disneyland; instead, you must purchase Disney Premier Access via the official website, official app, or third-party vendor like KLOOK.

Disney Premier Access:

- One Attraction for HKD 79 (about USD 10) is exclusively accessible through the official website and app.

- Choose three of the five well-liked rides for HKD 159 (HKD 150, or roughly USD 19.95), with Disney Premier Access - 3 Attractions.

- Disney Premier Access - 8 Attractions - HKD 329 (HKD 311 with the KLOOK discount, or roughly USD 41.25)

- Disney Premier Pass - "Momentous," including 8 attractions and 2 shows, costs HKD 549 (about USD 70.12; accessible exclusively on the official website and app).

priority admission to eight attractions, including a special viewing location for three performances, including the castle shows "Follow Your Dreams," "Momentous," and "Nighttime Spectacular."

The FastPass system that was once free has long since expired. Since Disney Parks across the world reopened, many of the parks have discontinued the FastPass free system and introduced line-skipping payment options on a recurring basis. Disney Genie+ for US Disney Parks and Disney Premier Access for overseas Disney Parks include the two main categories of the new systems.

If you think Individual Lightning Lane and Genie+ are hard, wait till you see how many Disney Premier Access options are offered at other Disney Parks across the world. When making travel plans to Hong Kong Disneyland, keep in mind that Disney Premier Access functions differently at each Disney park, so your past experiences at Disney World or Disneyland Resort will not carry over. On the plus side, though, you will experience the park in a "whole new way."

Different approaches are used by each park for its paid skip-the-line features; some are akin to Universal Studios' Express Passes and others to Individual Lightning Lane. The good news is that, in order to guarantee a space on a ride, most Disney Premier Access options do not need visitors to wake up at 7 am or to continuously check their phones. Nonetheless, several theme parks, such as Shanghai Disneyland and Hong Kong Disneyland, mandate that visitors conduct extensive research prior to making a purchase.

Here is the current status of Hong Kong Disneyland's FastPass systems without further ado.

Ways to Get Around the Line at Hong Kong Disneyland
For many years, three attractions at Disneyland were covered by the free paper FastPass. Nevertheless, the park also debuted the Priority Special Pass, an alternative premium FastPass variant, sometime between 2016 and 2017. For an extra charge, this pass permitted visitors to avoid the queue at some attractions.

When Hong Kong Disneyland eventually reopened on April 21, 2022, following a protracted hiatus due to the epidemic, visitors could only use the Disney Premier Access pass—basically, a rebranded Priority Special pass—as a skip-the-line option. The precise rationale for discontinuing the paper FastPass and Priority Special Pass is unknown, but it is certain that Hong Kong Disneyland is now solely focused on its Disney Premier Access pass as the main means for visitors to avoid lineups and make the most of their time in the park.

The FastPass system that was once free has long since expired. Since Disney Parks across the world reopened, many of the parks have discontinued the FastPass free system and introduced line-skipping payment options on a recurring basis. Disney Genie+ for US Disney Parks and Disney Premier Access for overseas Disney Parks include the two main categories of the new systems.

If you think Individual Lightning Lane and Genie+ are hard, wait till you see how many Disney Premier Access options are offered at other Disney Parks across the world. When making travel plans to Hong Kong Disneyland, keep in mind that Disney Premier Access functions differently at each Disney park, so your past experiences at Disney World or Disneyland Resort will not carry over. On the plus side, though, you will experience the park in a "whole new way."

Disneyland Hong Kong Disney Premier Access

Different approaches are used by each park for its paid skip-the-line features; some are akin to Universal Studios' Express Passes and others to Individual Lightning Lane. The good news is that, in order to guarantee a space on a ride, most Disney Premier Access options do not need visitors to wake up at 7 am or to continuously check their phones. Nonetheless, several theme parks, such as Shanghai Disneyland and Hong Kong Disneyland, mandate that visitors conduct extensive research prior to making a purchase.

Disney Premier Access

Chapter 4

ATTRACTIONS IN DISNEYLAND, HONG KONG

Disneyland Castle of Magical Dreams in Hong Kong

Hong Kong Disneyland Castle is one of the park's highlights. All of the Disney princesses—Snow White, Cinderella, Aurora, Ariel, Belle, Jasmine, Pocahontas, Mulan, Tiana, Rapunzel, Merida, Moana and Anna, and Elsa—as well as their pursuit of their ambitions are honoured in this one and only Disney castle.

Visitors to the park may notice details while strolling about the castle that bring back memories of their favourite heroine's plot. There's a Bibbidi Bobbidi Boutique at Storybook Shoppe. See the "Momentus" nightly extravaganza, which features lights, lasers, music, and synchronised fountains all around the castle.

On November 21, 2020, the castle opened to commemorate the park's 15th anniversary. In a past life, it was known as Sleeping Beauty Castle.

The Seven Themed Lands: Attractions, Dining, and Rides

The Hong Kong Disneyland app is among the greatest resources for information on the park. Its map is available for reference, but you should also check it for the park schedule and any closed attractions.

USA'S MAIN STREET
From an architectural standpoint, the Main Street U.S.A. buildings at Disneyland in California and Hong Kong are the same. The distinction is in the stories that are interwoven, suitably, with the park's Hong Kong setting.

It appears to be small-town America in the 20th century. The Emporium and other great souvenir stores are situated here.

Duffy and other plush stuffed animals like Tsum Tsums and Ufufy are hugely popular in Hong Kong. In fact, within the Main Street Cinema store here, you can see Duffy, ShellieMay, Gelatoni, and StellaLou.

Rides and Features:

- The Art of Animation at Animation Academy

- Main Street U.S.A. Station on the Hong Kong Disneyland Railroad Main Street Vehicles

- There's a grassy rotunda where you enter Main Street U.S.A., and there's typically a character welcoming going on. We avoid the queue here since it can get lengthy due to its proximity to the park entrance and instead wait for other Disney character greetings.

EAT: Enjoying the cuisine in Disneyland is a big part of the fun! The Corner Cafe serves afternoon tea, set dinners, and a respectable assortment of pastas and salads. Nothing special; it's just fine. Grab a delicious pastry or sandwich to go from Market House Bakery (which also has a Starbucks inside, if you like to collect these mugs emblazoned with the logo of Hong Kong Disneyland).

Should you desire table service For excellent cantonese cuisine, particularly dim sum, visit Plaza Inn, which is owned by the well-known company Jade Garden. Additionally, Cha Cha Room serves Chinese comfort food inside.

- Hong Kong Disneyland's dessert is an egg waffle with cream.

- In Hong Kong, egg waffles are a must-try.

- There are outdoor tables nearby as well as a snack cart with waffles, turkey drumsticks, and other goodies. A few visits ago, we picked up the egg waffle with cream shown above.

DREAMLAND
Imaginerland in Hong Kong It's a Small World, Dumbo, and other well-known rides can be found at Disneyland.
It's true that Dumbo frequently has some of the longest lines.

The happiest place for small children to be is Fantasyland, where you can stroll from Main Street U.S.A. via the Hong Kong Disneyland castle and find all the rides in close proximity.

Rides and Features:

- Presenting by Pandora is Cinderella's Carousel, Dumbo the Flying Elephant Fairytale Forest.

- Fantasyland Station on the Hong Kong Disneyland Railroad

- "It's a small world"—if there is a queue at all—moves extremely swiftly.

- Cups of Mad Hatters Tea

- The Multiverse Explorations of Winnie the Poo

- Mickey's PhilharMagic is a charming 4D presentation that is best suited for younger children.

- Disney characters can occasionally be seen at Sword in the Stone, but generally, it's just a phoney sword in a stone.

- Character greetings take place in Fantasy Gardens. There are lovely benches to sit on, and it is somewhat shaded. There are pagodas all across the yard, and inside are characters.

Although they will also use your camera, a professional photographer is available on-site to capture images for sale.

EAT: There are four stations at Royal Banquet Hall: International, Guangdong, Japanese, and Grill. When we previously dined here, the kids liked the sushi, dim sum, and other dishes. I was really impressed by the quality of what I got.

This is better than the terrible Chinese at Clopin's Festival of Food, in my opinion. Typically, Clopin's has imitation plates on display at the door to give you a visual representation of the meal. (The Explorer's Club in Mystic Point is a great place to go if you like Asian food; however, they don't provide Chinese food.)

- The ice cream shop beside the "it's a small world" exit is also great, though it hasn't been open lately.

- Inside Hong Kong Disneyland's Toy Story Land, visitors stroll about.

- This land, which is conveniently close to Fantasyland, is modelled after the well-known Toy Story films.

Rides and Features:

- Fun-Packed RC Racer Slinky Dog Spin (essential for small children)

- Toy Soldier Parachute Drop: Despite having one of the nicest views in the park and a terrific ride, the queue moves slowly.

- Before boarding the Toy Soldier Parachute Drop, you will be asked to place your purses and personal items in a cubby. A DSLR is too bulky, but if you have a smartphone on a neck strap or a GoPro attached to you, the view just before the parachute drops is fairly amazing (weather permitting).

EAT: The only place to get drinks and snack items, such as soft serve with boba, is here at Jessie's Snack Roundup. The snacks appear to change frequently, but on our most recent visit, we had the pineapple frozen drink, which is somewhat of like

Dole Whip but with pandan and soft serve. This is our go-to spot for exciting sweets every time.

- The dessert similar to a Dole Whip at Hong Kong Disneyland

- Hong Kong Disneyland's Churro Soft Serve Ice Cream is served in Jessie's Snack Shack.

- A snack cart owned by Jessie at Hong Kong Disneyland

EXCLUSIVE TO HONG KONG DISNEYLAND: MYSTIC POINT

The newest land to debut at Hong Kong Disneyland is called Mystic Point, and it's exclusive to that park.

Mystic Manor is the one and only ride that is not to be missed. Although it has a completely different plot and far more advanced special effects than the well-known Haunted Mansion ride, it is stylistically comparable to it.

The façade of Mystic Manor is one of Hong Kong Disneyland's greatest rides.

The outside of Mystic Manor.

In the centre of a vast, unexplored rainforest in Papua New Guinea, this territory is home to an explorer by the name of Lord Henry Mystic, who resides there (in Mystic Manor, of course) and is the scene of mysterious forces and supernatural events.

Rides and Features:

- Garden of Enchantment

- Mystic Manor—among the park's greatest rides, with amazing special effects and Danny Elfman's music.

- Mystic Point Freight Depot (a location where children can explore and stroll around)

EAT: The greatest restaurant at Hong Kong Disneyland is The Explorer's Club Restaurant. Southeast Asian, Japanese, Korean, and Indonesian cuisine is served at various counter-order stations here. I frequently have delicious Hainanese chicken rice, and my daughter just had a bento box that was really tasty as well.

The only tricky part is that you have to wait in queue twice if you want Southeast Asian food and your kids prefer Japanese (which happens to me occasionally and isn't too bothersome). There are five dining rooms in this Hong Kong Disneyland restaurant, each with a different theme from across the globe. Additionally, every dish on the menu is halal.

The Explorer's Club's Hainan chicken rice is the best restaurant in Hong Kong Disneyland, in my view.
Rice with Hainanese chicken at the Explorer's Club eatery
Although it's not Michelin-star level, the park's food has become better with time.

- Hong Kong Disneyland's Mystic Point features a frozen dessert cart.

- There's a frozen dessert snack cart at Mystic Point as well. These delights must be consumed immediately (and with lots of napkins) because they melt easily in the summer.

BITTER GULCH
The Dumbo owned by my daughter pokes his head out of the Grizzly Gulch photo area at Hong Kong Disneyland.
Location for Grizzly Gulch photos

Frontierland in Hong Kong Disneyland is modelled after the Wild West of the 19th century and is called Grizzly Gulch.

It's modest, with just one ride, Big Grizzly Mountain Runaway Mine Cars, a roller coaster modelled after Disneyland Anaheim's Big Thunder Mountain Railroad.

This is my favourite ride in the whole park and a great way to introduce younger children to roller coasters. We've brought a few of my daughter's timid friends along for the ride, and they thoroughly enjoyed it.

It changes at one point from a high forward speed to a high but controllable backward speed, which makes it unique. The launch of the ride is very cool.

Grizzly Gulch is easy to stroll through the remainder of.

Attractions and rides:

- Large Grizzly Mountain Mine Cars Escape Geyser Gulch Fun Shots in the Wild West

EAT: A snack shop and a popcorn cart are available.

- Advancing Land

- Mandarin, Cantonese, and English are the languages spoken during the Jungle Cruise trips at Hong Kong Disneyland.

- Never pass up the Jungle Cruise.

- Like me, you probably love Disney, so you'll be happy to hear that this Adventureland is the biggest one in all of the Disney Parks.

RIDES & ATTRACTIONS

- Jungle River Cruise (signs based on language show where to queue)

- Karibuni Marketplace: an area where characters frequently congregate

- Liki Tikis: not so much a ride but an interactive water play area

- Tarzan's Treehouse via Rafts

- The Treehouse of Tarzan

EAT: Korean squid, turkey legs, and other snacks are available at these two snack carts. Here, you may also obtain freshly cut fruit. Southeast Asian food is served quickly at Tahitian Terrace.

TOMORROWLAND

The park's most popular attraction is now located on this land, which is undergoing the biggest transformation.

At Hong Kong Disneyland, where some of the greatest rides, such Hyperspace Mountain and Buzz

Lightyear Astro Blasters, are located, my daughter "holds up" the Tomorrowland globe.
The enormous Tomorrowland Sign After turning off Main Street U.S.A., you will arrive in Tomorrowland.

Rides and Features:

- Ant-Man vs. Wasp: Nano Conflict!

- Hyperspace Mountain, which is actually Space Mountain with a Star Wars theme

- Experience Iron Man with Orbitron

- Stark Industries presents the Iron Man Tech Showcase at the Star Wars Command Post.

Recently, my daughter and her pals went to Star Wars Command Post for Jedi training. They found the theatrics entertaining, although they were a touch too old for it at ten. Cantonese is used in the show.

Younger children could enjoy Hong Kong Disneyland's interactive Star Wars Command Post show. It is essentially training for Jedi. My daughter in the show with a few of her pals.

Being unique to this park and the first Disney attraction based on a Marvel character, Iron Man Experience is a huge deal. It's fantastic.

I adore how important Hong Kong buildings are included throughout the trip (which, to be honest, those who have just arrived would not recognise).

This is a description of the ride.

Tony Stark, the renowned inventor and trailblazer, has chosen Tomorrowland at Hong Kong Disneyland to hold Stark Expo. at these exhibition halls—the Hall of Legacy, the Hall of Protection, the Hall of Energy, and the Hall of Mobility—he will showcase his most recent high-tech achievements. In the Iron Man Experience, guests will be among the first to get a close-up look at Tony Stark's most recent inventions and experience flying in a gravity-defying Iron Wing vehicle. Additionally, he designated Hong Kong as Stark Industries' future Asia headquarters.

The park invested more than three years in designing and building the Iron Man Experience, which includes flying simulators, surround sound, 3-D projection, and other special effects to fully immerse visitors in the Marvel tale of a conflict with Hydra's villainous forces.

January 2017 saw the arrival of the all-new Iron Man Experience at Hong Kong Disneyland.
The image is courtesy of Hong Kong Disneyland. Ant-Man and the Wasp: Nano Battle! is the character's first attraction. Additionally, it's the first Marvel attraction in a Disney Park with a female superhero serving as the main character.

Although it replaces Buzz Lightyear Astro Blasters, this attraction is comparable in that riders shoot targets in an attempt to achieve the best score.

Futureland shutdowns: In order to create room for the Iron Man Experience, Autopia was removed in addition to Buzz Lightyear Astro Blasters. Too bad, because in the US, we drive on the left, I thought the right-drive cars were hilarious.

EAT: For an American-style burger, a basket of chicken fingers, and other such fare, the Starlight Diner is the greatest spot in the park.

Starlight Diner cuisine at Hong Kong Disneyland
The menu for Starlight Diner

Kids will enjoy the space-themed design, the counter ordering tends to flow rapidly, and they have a large dining area. Also, there is a well-liked popcorn cart with a variety of flavours and a BB-8 snack cart that serves decent ice cream.

The Top 10 Rides in Hong Kong Disneyland

The following rides at Hong Kong Disneyland are our favourites:

- Large Runaway Mine Cars in Grizzly Mountain (Grizzly Gulch)

- Mount Hyperspace (Tomorrowland)

- Mystic Point, or Mystic Manor

- Tomorrowland's Ant-Man and the Wasp: Nano Battle

- The Tomorrowland Experience of Iron Man

- Parachute Drop of the Toy Soldier from Toy Story Land

- It's a Fantasyland that's little.

- Disneyworld's Dumbo the Flying Elephant

- Adventureland's Jungle River Cruise (Toy Story Land) RC Racer

You can handle this whole list and then some on a normal day.

How to Reduce The Wait Times for Rides
Note: During times when the park is at capacity, this advise is primarily relevant when there are crowds.

- Similar to other Disney theme parks, the best way to avoid crowds is to visit the park as soon as it opens on a weekday that isn't a holiday. It's what we do, and we can just stroll on and off of the rides.

- A few years ago, we did go during the busiest time of year—August—for the holidays. The weather was oppressively hot and swarming with mainland tourists. Although the crowds have somewhat subsided at the new Shanghai Disneyland, they will probably persist during school breaks like these.

- One of the most popular attractions, Dumbo, had a 25-minute wait when it was deemed congested during a recent Easter week. I didn't think 25 minutes was a huge problem because I had just visited Shanghai Disneyland, where wait times topped three hours.

- By the standards of Hong Kong Disneyland, this is "long." The Toy Soldier Parachute Drop is the one exception; in any season, there may be a wait of up to an hour. This attraction in Hong Kong Disneyland is, in my opinion, the slowest queue in the whole park.

- In the event that one member of your party is unable to ride, remember to use Rider Switch. While the other adult bikes, one adult waits in a pre-designated area with a child. The grownups can then trade places.

- DOWNLOAD THE Disney app for Hong Kong.

- The Hong Kong Disneyland app allows you to make reservations, view a GPS-enabled map, find out when and where characters will appear, estimate wait times at specific attractions, and access a host of other information. You really must get this app for free.

Animation Standby Pass
You can use the app to obtain a Disney Standby Pass for a few attractions once you enter the park. After choosing an attraction, your party will be given a time slot to visit. At the moment, character meet & greets are covered by this.

- Main Street Cinema with Lina Bell

- Entire royal family gathered at The Royal Reception Hall.

- Character Meeting at The Annex: An Exclusive Offer for Magic Access Members

- Disney Premiere Pass Entrance

- Disney Premier Access comes in two varieties, which you may buy online ahead of time or at the park. Walk-up purchase locations are subject to change and are established by the resort.

- Disney occasionally offers specials for 10% off, so it makes sense to purchase your Premier Access pass online. Advanced purchasing is only available online.

- With these passes, visitors can skip the queue and enter the rides faster. It's crucial to understand that although this line is shorter than the main one, lines for popular rides like Iron Man can still last up to 20 minutes.

- You can choose three of the following attractions to receive one-time priority access to with Disney Premier – 3 Attractions (HKD 159):

- The Great Grizzly Mountain Escape Mine Vehicles

- Ant-Man vs. Wasp: Nano Conflict!

- The Iron Man Experience at Mystic Manor

- A little planet, that is

- Disney Premier Access-Eight Attractions (HKD 329) offers prioritised one-time entry to:

- The Great Grizzly Mountain Escape Mine Vehicles

- Ant-Man vs. Wasp: Nano Conflict!

- Iron Man Experience at Mystic Manor: Small world, huh?

- Winnie the Pooh's Many Adventures Toy Soldier Parachute Drop Slinky Dog Spin

You won't get a price break or an additional Premier Access entry if one of these rides is closed. The last time we visited Toy Soldier Parachute Drop, it was closed.

Priority Admission Pass (formerly known as Disney Premier Access) admission at the Toy Soldiers Parachute Drop ride at Hong Kong Disneyland allows riders to bypass even the often "long" Fast Pass queue.

The Follow Your Dreams guided tour is the name of the VIP tour offered by Hong Kong Disneyland. As of this writing, the cost for up to six persons is HKD 5988 (about USD 728), and park admission is not included.

- Direct access to the rides of your choosing and privileged seats at performances are included in this VIP tour.

- Although I have reserved the Shanghai Disneyland VIP Tour, I have never needed this tour. It is something to think about for peace of mind in case you are concerned about possible crowds, or for summer weekends, August, and Chinese New Year. Additionally, it will be useful to avoid standing in line in the sweltering summer heat.

Other Hong Kong Disneyland Advice: What to Pack, Facilities, and More.

Arrive at Hong Kong Disneyland just before it opens to witness the ritual that is shown in this picture.

At least fifteen minutes before opening, visitors will be allowed to enter the park all the way to the end of Main Street, USA.

- GET HERE PRIOR TO THE PARK OPENING

- To get to the end of Main Street U.S.A. before the park officially opens, guests may enter through the turnstiles at least fifteen minutes early (maybe sooner, but I've never tried).

- Observing the opening ceremony, in which a child or family of choice cuts the ribbon with scissors, is one motivation to do this.

- The primary reason, though, is that you'll be in a fantastic position to get to your favourite ride first because you'll be thus far into the park. I advise you to visit Tomorrowland to see Iron Man or Ant-Man, or Toy Story Land to see the Toy Soldier Parachute Drop.

What To Pack And Guidelines

Remember to bring insect repellent and sunblock. The latter is particularly helpful if you want to stay up late.

If you're going in the summer, pack a travel umbrella for shade and a hand-held fan (the latter will probably be a nice, Disney-branded fan that will cost more in the park if it's hot). Nowadays, I use a USB fan that connects to my phone; nonetheless, water-spritzing fans come in quite helpful during Hong Kong summers.

It is not allowed for you to bring in outside food or beverages. It is not permitted for adults over 16 to wear costume masks. Skates, scooters, and shoes with wheels are prohibited, as are selfie sticks. Go over the remaining guidelines and restrictions for the park.

TAKING OFF A STROLLER

Having carried a Bugaboo pram on several occasions, I never experienced any problems leaving it in any location at Hong Kong Disneyland while I rode a ride.

I never left anything expensive inside, though, so you should proceed at your own risk. At the park, stroller rentals are also offered.

Disney Persona Salutations

Greeting Pluto at Hong Kong Disneyland with my 2-year-old daughter.

You can say hello to characters on every land in the park. Because so many people enter the park here and become extremely thrilled to see Mickey, Minnie, and their friends, there are usually large lineups at the Town Square welcomes in Main Street U.S.A.

I would advise avoiding this welcome section. To locate additional characters to meet, using the Hong Kong Disneyland app. For example, you can frequently find the Disney Princesses at Royal Princess Garden.

Characters frequently sign autograph books, which are available for purchase in Main Street's Emporium. It's a great memento for your kids to have from their exciting park day. They can also add stickers to this book that they get from park employees.

DINING WITH CHARACTER AND PRINCESS ATTIRE

The Hong Kong Disneyland Hotel is home to the Bibbidi Bobbidi Boutique, which is situated outside of Hong Kong Disneyland.
Make reservations for character dinner at a Hong Kong Disneyland Hotel when it's pouring outside.
The Disneyland Resort Hotels in Hong Kong provide character dining. Usually, you can find them here (be sure to check before you travel).

Mickey Mouse, Minnie Mouse, and other characters can be seen at the character-filled supper and breakfast buffets at Enchanted Garden (Hong Kong Disneyland Hotel) (lunch buffet only on weekends). Out of all the character dining options, this is the most expensive.

Dragon Wind (Disney Explorer's Lodge): This Chinese restaurant serves a character dining lunch buffet on weekends and public holidays, as well as a character dining breakfast buffet with regional and Western options.

World of Colour (Disney Explorer's Lodge): A global assortment of breakfast buffet items are served alongside Donald and Goofy dressed as Explorers at breakfast.

Disney's Hollywood Hotel's Chef Mickey: Mickey Mouse dons chef attire and strikes a portrait at the breakfast buffet.

There is now a Bibbidi Bobbidi Boutique housed at the Hong Kong Disneyland Hotel. The kids will want to go to the park after if you stay at the Hong Kong Disneyland Hotel Bibbidi Bobbidi Boutique, so make plans for that.

DISNEYLAND HONG KONG VS OTHER DISNEYLANDS?

Among the theme parks I have been to, Hong Kong Disneyland is undoubtedly the most unique. Many of the classic faves are there, although they frequently have a twist, like (Hyper)space Mountain. It has a lot of attractions that I had never seen before. I particularly enjoyed how heavily the Iron Man Adventure featured Hong Kong themes. Seeing Hong Kong in that light was enjoyable.

- It is evident that Hong Kong Disneyland is the newest Disneyland I have been to. The rides have been upgraded and made more modern, which explains some of the variations I noticed. This is a huge benefit for Disneyland in Hong Kong.

- For us, the most benefit of all was the significantly reduced number of people. Compared with my previous park visits, this one was far more enjoyable.

- Although we were in this park over the Easter school vacations, so it may have contributed in part, I believe that generally speaking it is a less crowded area to visit. Numerous friends have informed me that they have visited without even needing to wait in queue!

- We never waited in queue longer than 20 minutes anyplace over the majority of the day, and queue lengths never exceeded 30 minutes. There were rides with no queue at all. The longest wait was 50 minutes, and that was only for one ride, even when we departed during peak hours. For me, this is really a different experience!

- The park uses a lot of English, which I really liked. Speaking no local language made us feel like we were missing out on a lot, in contrast to my visit to Tokyo Disneyland where I found that much of the information was in Japanese.

- There didn't seem to be as many live performances, which was something I did not particularly enjoy. The parades were about the only thing going on. It's nice to have a reason to take a seat, unwind, and be entertained for a little while.

- The diminutive Sleeping Beauty's Castle was the only other unfavourable change I could find. This is typically the park's signature attraction, but on this occasion it wasn't as good.

- Taking the family to Hong Kong Disneyland?

- We went on our Hong Kong Disney review with our three children, who were five, six, and ten months old.

- Our assessment of Disneyland Hong Kong revealed that it's a great place to take kids, as we had anticipated! We knew we loved it when they did!

- Much though I adored Disneyland before having children, witnessing my children's amazement makes it much more memorable. Because there were fewer people here, we also found Disneyland to be quite accessible and simple to visit.

- While many rides do have a minimum height requirement, it is typically 102 cm. Our just turned five-year-old was able to do everything he wanted.

- It was undoubtedly more difficult to visit Disneyland with a newborn, and the experience made me realise why, in the past, I had only brought our oldest child and left our toddler Z with my spouse. Because there isn't much for a baby to do, one adult is usually left behind to take care of baby J. Positively, he was unrestricted.

- The fact that I only learned that "rider switch" is permitted at the park right before we departed is really inconvenient. Here, you can both queue with your non-riding youngster and alternately take turns riding the ride while the other adult tends to your child. This eliminates the need for you to queue all over again after one adult has completed the ride (which is what we did for the more challenging rides!).

- I wish this had been known to us earlier! The map has it printed there in small letters. They advise asking attraction employees if you wish to do this.

- The park is great for strollers. You may rent one, but we brought our own. There are plenty of places to park strollers, and each stroller comes with a strap that you can personalise with your name. Throughout the park, there is a baby care centre and change tables.

- When visiting with children, another item to watch out for is staff stickers. Your children can approach staff members and request them.

Chapter 5

HOTELS IN DISNEYLAND, HONG KONG

1. Hong Kong Disneyland Hotel

Advantages of Booking Accommodations at Hong Kong Disneyland

There are significant differences between the three hotels at Hong Kong Disneyland. I wouldn't claim that one is superior to the other in every case. Which you select will rely on your spending limit and desired experience. We have stayed in all of them, so I can describe their merits with accuracy.

SPECIAL DISCOUNTS FOR HOTEL GUESTS

Hotel guests in Hong Kong Disneyland used to have benefits, but that has changed! They are also worthwhile.

At the park's Main Entrance, hotel guests have access to a special "Disney Hotel Guests Entrance." There is no early park entry for hotel guests.

As an additional convenient mode of transportation, visitors can take the free resort shuttle from any of the three hotels to the Disneyland Resort Public Transport Interchange.

Character appearances, Disney-themed hotel activities, and enchanted playrooms all contribute to the Disney joy of staying at the Disneyland hotels. While infant facilities like cots and bathtubs make it simple to care for the small ones, guests can explore the hotel gardens in search of hidden Mickeys or take a stroll along the seaside promenade.

A themed suite, like the Frozen suite at Kingdom's Club, the Cinderella suite at Hong Kong Disneyland Hotel, or the Avengers suite at Disney Explorers Lodge, can make for an especially memorable experience.

You can also receive a free drink and a room upgrade from standard to deluxe when you book online.

The hotels' distance to Hong Kong Disneyland.
Hong Kong Disneyland's front entrance has directional signage.
Remarks on the hotels There's a handy bus that goes from the hotels to the park. Although most people don't, you can stroll from the Hong Kong Disneyland hotels to the theme park.

Both hotels are busy, so in my opinion, you don't get the same level of personal attention as you would in a hotel of a comparable price in another area of Hong Kong. Having said that, we typically spend at least one night at Hong Kong Disneyland when my daughter and I travel there.

2. Disney's Hotel Hollywood

Disney's Hollywood Hotel at Hong Kong Disneyland is a great option.

Disney's Hollywood Hotel, with its Art Deco design, is the most affordable choice. Nonetheless, I thought it was reasonably priced. The spacious grassy spaces, laid-back atmosphere, and pool shaped like a piano will appeal to children.

Here you may have character breakfast and supper (the timing and dates of the latter are subject to change), and the food is quite good. Although comfortable, standard rooms are fairly colourful. For additional information, see our comprehensive evaluation of the Disney's Hollywood Hotel.

3. Lodge for Disney Explorers

The newest hotel at Hong Kong Disneyland is called Disney Explorers Lodge.

In April 2017, the 750-room Disney Explorers Lodge, designed like a resort, opened. It is priced between Disney's Hollywood Hotel and Hong Kong Disneyland Hotel and is furnished to reflect the four distinct tropical climates of Asia, Oceania, South America, and Africa.

Hotel Disneyland in Hong Kong
Although it isn't as luxurious as the amazing five-star hotels found across Hong Kong, this hotel is still a great choice. Though not very lavish, the accommodations are decent and somewhat better than Disney's Hollywood Hotel, with a Victorian aesthetic reminiscent of Orlando's Grand Floridian.

Bibbidi Bobbidi Boutique, more upscale character restaurants, and the excellent Cantonese restaurant Crystal Lotus (which serves Disney dim sum) are all housed in this hotel.

The accommodations provide pleasant views of the South China Sea, a kid-friendly hedge maze, and a swimming pool. Although I haven't yet, I will soon write a review of this motel.

Staying at the resort is highly recommended if you want to fully experience everything Disney and take advantage of all the amenities it has to offer.

You could easily spend the same amount of money or less on a nicer hotel in Central or Kowloon, as the park is so conveniently accessible (details below). We frequently stay at the Four Seasons Hotel Hong Kong and the Mandarin Oriental Hong Kong. Both are conveniently located in Central and kid-friendly, but Hong Kong has an abundance of amazing hotels, some of the best in the world, really.

Keep Inspiration Lake Recreation Centre in Mind
This charming neighbourhood in Hong Kong is a hidden treasure, especially during the mild months. Yes, that is a lake, and the park is surrounded by woodlands. Inspiration Lake is a lovely location for fitness, strolling, and a change of scenery. Admission is free. You can rent pedal boats and bikes from Surrey. A snack store is also present.

Alternatively, you can go to Tsing Yi station on the Airport Express and change to the Tung Chung line there. To get to Sunny Bay station, take Tung Chung. From there, take the Disneyland Resort Line to the park. About thirty-five minutes will pass.

Expect Cultural Differences

Most of the visitors are from mainland China and are residents of Hong Kong. Compared to Disney Parks in the United States, there is a significantly higher adult to child ratio.

KIDS: Since this style is still uncommon on the mainland, your youngster may draw notice if they have light coloring. My daughter has pale white complexion, blue eyes, and strawberry blonde hair. Very friendly mainland Chinese people frequently stop her and complement her features or want to snap a picture with her.

LINE CUTTING: In contrast to the civility I just discussed, line cutting does occur. Locals in Hong Kong are keen to point out that these individuals are not from the country. Line-cutting incidents have decreased recently, but to keep individuals from getting through, I advise you to stand in queue with a purpose and a broad stance, if that makes sense.

FOOD: I had a hamburger at Starlight Diner when Hong Kong Disneyland first opened. It had a bun, a patty, mayonnaise, and raw cucumber slices that were meant to represent pickles in the American way. Since then, the burger situation has improved. My point is that you should always keep in mind that you are in Asia and that Western food may not look or taste exactly how it does at home.

Control your children's expectations so they don't become excited about seeing and eating foods that aren't typical for them but are for youngsters in other countries. One of the things I enjoy most about travelling and visiting Disney Parks all around the world is encouraging them to try something new. Starlight Diner is the greatest option if you're looking for the most Westernised cuisine selections.

STAYING OFF-SITE

One of the three on-site hotels can be pricey, so it might not be ideal for everyone's tastes or budget. Thankfully, there are still pleasant and convenient off-site lodging choices available. If you stay in downtown Hong Kong, you may experience more of the city's attractions and culture. By taxi or public transit, you may easily get to the park and take in the sights and sounds of Hong Kong on the way.

If you investigate hotels and locate one that fits your needs and budget, staying off-site during your visit to Hong Kong Disneyland is not a bad idea. Even if you choose to stay off-site, you may still have an amazing time visiting the park and discover the finest of Hong Kong.

Chapter 6

HONG KONG DINING AND CUISINE

Hong Kong is known as a "Gourmet Heaven" for its fine and mouthwatering cuisine, in addition to being a "Shopping Paradise" and "Commercial Centre." Every district in the area offers a diverse selection of mouthwatering foreign eating alternatives, so visit Hong Kong and indulge in a gastronomic adventure you won't soon forget!

Fantastic Hong Kong cuisine is ready to provide you with an unforgettable trip to Hong Kong! Hong Kong, being an international city, offers a diverse range of dining experiences influenced by many cultures and preferences. All visitors are welcome to savor delectable five-star meals, as well as casual neighborhood fare, at Eastern and Western Hong Kong restaurants including Thai, Vietnamese, Indian, Mediterranean, Japanese, French, and Italian eateries. The visitors have a variety of dining options at the unique restaurants. Let's use TravelKing to discover the cuisine of Hong Kong!

Hong Kong's Three Most Famous Culinary Districts

Recognised as Asia's culinary epicenter, Hong Kong features over 11,000 eateries arranged throughout several neighborhoods. Hong Kong's most popular dining areas are Causeway Bay, Tsim Sha Tsui, and Kowloon.

渚澍 KOWLOON

One of Hong Kong's most well-liked neighborhoods for foodies, Kowloon was once an industrial neighborhood but has now transformed into a residential neighborhood with a plethora of South East Asian and international cuisines, Cantonese and Chiu Chow meals, and local snacks and desserts. Small eateries with amiable staff may be found by visitors. Nga Tsin Long Road, Nam Kwok Road, Lung Kong Road, Prince Edward Road, Kai Tak Road, and Fuk Lo Tsun Road are the primary routes where the eateries are situated. Don't forget to stop at the neighborhood eateries and cafés along the way.

尖沙咀 TSUI TSIM SHA

Kowloon's Tsim Sha Tsui is a vibrant neighborhood for foodies. Many international four- and five-star hotels are conveniently located and have the best restaurants with breathtaking views of the harbor and Hong Kong Island across the sea. Along Hillwood Road, Nathan Road, Canton Road, Chatham Road, Ashley Road, and Cameron Road, savor delectable cuisine prepared by some of the best chefs in the world.

銅鑼灣 CAUSEWAY BAY

For a true taste of Hong Kong, travelers may get a variety of affordable local specialties at Causeway Bay. Along Tang Lung, Matheson, and Jardine's

Bazaar streets, you can get delicacies that are locally made. The famous Hong Kong style tea, which appeals to all diners with its appealing aroma, is served at neighborhood eateries and stalls. Yun Ping Road, Kai Chiu Road, Pak Sha Road, Lan Fong Road, Hysan Avenue, Sunning Road, Hoi Ping Road, and Yiu Wa Street are all delicious options for an evening out if you're looking for great cuisine.

You also shouldn't miss Lan Kwai Fong & SOHO, Hung Hom, Sai Kung, Lei Yue Mun, and Lamma Island, which are other important cuisine districts in Hong Kong.

Famous Hong Kong Delights

Which Snacks And Specialties From Hong Kong Should You Not Miss?

Dim Sum //
You must try dim sum if you are visiting Hong Kong! For breakfast or lunch, dum sum is a wonderful, flavorful Chinese snack that is served in

steaming bamboo baskets with pots of Chinese tea on the side. The popular dim sum dishes in the area, such as pan-fried squid, shrimp dumplings, steamed pork buns, streamed pig ribs and beef balls, will definitely entice you to stay!

REGIONAL STREET FOOD 料式小吃

Hong Kong indigenous street foods include curry fish balls, beef balls, sausages, squid tentacles, fried veggies, and more. They are offered in Styrofoam bowls or on sticks so that people can eat them while traveling to their destination. The meat and fish balls in curry have a robust flavor and are juicy.

FISH AND SEAFOOD

For those who adore seafood and are gluttons, Hong Kong is nirvana! Fresh fish served Hong Kong-style by talented Cantonese chefs. The islands of Lamma and Cheung Chau, Sai Kung, and Lei Yue Mun are the top four seafood areas for dining by the waterfront.

BBQ IN CANTONESE 港式懶燜

Cantonese BBQ meals include roast duck, cha siu, crispy roast pig, soy sauce chicken, and many other dishes with roast meat flavours. In Hong Kong, you can find these delicious Cantonese BBQ treats on every corner. Furthermore, two of the most well-known Cantonese BBQ restaurants in Hong Kong are Tai Xing Roast Restaurant and Hong Kong Yung Kee Restaurant. These eateries attracted a lot of foreign guests who came to sample their delectable offerings.

Chapter 7

HONG KONG THEMED TOURS

Asia's wonderland is Hong Kong.The city is home to numerous unique local blocks, well-known retail areas, and art museums. Well-known tourist destinations in Hong Kong are suggested for your trip there by Hong Kong tourism!

TOURS OF MUSEUMS

The Hong Kong Historical Museum
The Hong Kong Heritage Museum was founded with the purpose of showcasing a unique blend of art, culture, and history. With six permanent galleries—the Orientation Theatre, the New Territories Heritage Hall, the Cantonese Opera Heritage Hall, the T.T. Tsui Gallery of Chinese Art, the Chao Shao, and the Children's Discovery Gallery—and six themed galleries that occasionally feature a variety of Hong Kong treasures, the museum boasts a total exhibition area of 7,500 meters.

Location: Sha Tin, Hong Kong; No. 1 Man Lam Road.
Using the MTR: 1. Get off at Che Kung Temple Station, and then walk for five minutes.

2. Take a train to Sha Tin Station, and then stroll for fifteen minutes.

Museum of Coastal Defence in Hong Kong
The Hong Kong Museum of Coastal Defence, formerly known as the Lei Yue Mun Fort, played a

significant role in the 1941 Battle for Hong Kong. The history of coastal defense in China from the Ming and Qing Dynasties is shown by the museum. In a calm setting, visitors can examine the relics and artifacts and discover Hong Kong's past.

Location: Shau Kei Wan, Hong Kong; No. 175 Tung Hei Road
By MTR: Get off at Shau Kei Wan Station's Exit B2, then walk for fifteen minutes while following the signage on the road.
By Bus: Ride Citybus No. 85, which travels from Siu Sai Wan to North Point Ferry Piers.

Hong Kong Art Museum

The Hong Kong Museum of Art was founded in 1962 and now has a collection of 15,000 artworks, including pieces by local artists, calligraphic art, antique Chinese treasures, traditional Chinese paintings, and cultural relics. In addition to the priceless artwork, a vast array of educational programmes are available to broaden visitors' understanding and pique their enthusiasm in art.

Location: Tsim Sha Tsui, Kowloon, Hong Kong; No. 10 Salisbury Road

By MTR: Get out at Tsim Sha Tsui Station Exit E/J/K/L3.

By Ferry: Get off at Tsim Sha Tsui's Star Ferry Pier.

Hong Kong Historical Museum

Formerly called the Hong Kong Museum of History and Art, the Hong Kong Museum of History is located in Hong Kong. Later, it was divided into a distinct museum with an emphasis on history. Ninety thousand collections of natural history, folklore, archaeology, and local history are kept in storage at the Museum.

Location: Tsim Sha Tsui, Kowloon, Hong Kong; 100 Chatham Road South (near to the Hong Kong Science Museum)

By MTR: 1. Get off at Tsim Sha Tsui Station's exit B2, then stroll down Cameron Road. It takes roughly eighteen minutes to walk from the museum in the direction of Tsim Sha Tsui East.

2. Get off at Jordan Station Station's exit D, then go down Austin Road. It takes roughly twenty minutes to walk from the museum to Tsim Sha Tsui East.

3. Take a train to Hung Hom Station, then head towards Tsim Sha Tsui. The walk to the museum takes fifteen minutes.

Hong Kong Museum of Science
With more than 500 displays spread across 6,500 square metres of permanent exhibition space, about 70% of them are interactive and appropriate for visitors of all ages. Visitors can interact with and use high-tech products. The museum is a special and excellent location to study science.

Address: 2 Science Museum Road, Kowloon, Hong Kong's Tsimshatsui East
By MTR: 1. Get off at Tsim Sha Tsui Station's exit B2, then stroll down Cameron Road. It takes roughly eighteen minutes to walk from the museum in the direction of Tsim Sha Tsui East.

2. Get off at Jordan Station Station's exit D, then go down Austin Road. It takes roughly twenty minutes to walk from the museum to Tsim Sha Tsui East.

3. Take a train to Hung Hom Station, then head towards Tsim Sha Tsui. The walk to the museum takes fifteen minutes.

Hong Kong Museum of Space

The Hong Kong Space Museum, divided into East and West sides, is a distinctive edifice with an egg-shaped dome, making it one of the city's landmarks. The Stanley Ho Space Theatre, the Hall of Space Science, workshops, and offices are incorporated in the East side, which serves as the planetarium's central core. The Lecture Hall, the Hall of Astronomy, and the Gift Shop are located on the West side. If astronomy piques your interest, you are welcome to engage with the museum and take part in its programmes to learn more about space.

The address: is 10 Salisbury Road, Kowloon, Hong Kong, Tsim Sha Tsui.The Museum of Hong Kong Racing

Via MTR: The museum can be found next to the Tsim Sha Tsui MTR Station exit.

Museum of Hong Kong Racing

The Hong Kong Racing Museum tells tales of horse racing from 1840, including updated racing lanes and the historically large payout for a lottery winner, through eight exhibition galleries and a miniature movie theatre. You can get more familiar with Hong Kong horse racing with each exhibition.

Address: Happy Valley Stand, No. 2/F, Happy Valley, Hong Kong
By MTR: You can take the MTR to Times Square station's exit A to go to the museum.

REMINISCENT TOURS

In central western Hong Kong, there is a wide variety of tourism that emphasises modern, technology, heritage, and nostalgia. Indulge in vintage seafood shops and herbal medicine stores as well as learn more about Hong Kong's economic growth in recent years.

Market in the West
In addition to being the oldest surviving market building in Hong Kong, Western Market was constructed in 1960 using brick and granite. It is a

notable example of an Edwardian style construction. The market is a four-story structure that the Hong Kong government now officially recognises as a historical landmark. The market offers a broad selection of goods.

Street Wing Lok

A well-known spot to get ginseng and edible swallow bird's nest is Wing Lok Street. stores offering a range of dried seafood products, Chinese herbs, and medications. Wing Lok Street is a terrific spot to explore if you're looking for traditional Chinese nutrition in Hong Kong.

West Des Voeux Road
A historic street, Des Voeux Road West is lined with shops offering an extensive selection of Chinese medicine along with premium dried seafood, including bird's nest, shark fin, and abalone. It is advised of visitors to evaluate costs and make their purchase at the most affordable price.

Ko Shiing Road

One well-known Chinese medicine market is on Ko Shing Street. This location is where visitors can find a variety of valuable herbal medications, with Des Voeu Road West at the opposite end.

West of Bonham Strand (Nam Bug Hong)

Known for its dried seafood and Chinese herbs, Bonham Strand West (Nam Bug Hong) is situated in central Hong Kong, close to Sheung Wan and the Western Market. Although the stores are open to individuals, they function on a wholesale basis. The merchants can also instruct you on how to use and prepare dried seafood. Because every business on the street sells the same things, mostly in bulk, the prices could be reasonable. But the suppliers usually don't appreciate a good deal!

Hollywood Avenue

The Hollywood Road, which is in the heart of Hong Kong, is an antique lover's paradise! Numerous antique stores offering Chinese porcelain, furniture, rugs, pottery, memorabilia, and other items are lining the road. If you have an interest in antiques, you should not miss seeing Hollywood Road.

Row A Upper Lascar

Cat Street is another name for Upper Lascar Row, and Hollywood Road runs along its northern edge. Upper Lascar Row is a commercial hub for the antique trade, much like Hollywood Road. This place offers opulent artistic productions together with a variety of nostalgic commodities. Going to Upper Lascar Row is similar to travelling through a time machine to the past.

Man Mo Miu, or Man Mo Temple

Hong Kong's Man Mo Temple (Man Mo Miu) is home to the statues of Kwan Yu, the God of War, and Man Cheong, the God of Literature. The antique bronze bell and a comprehensive understanding of Chinese culture are the main draws for both Chinese and foreign visitors to the temple.

TOURS OF SHOPPING

BAY CAUSEWAY

Hong Kong's commercial and entertainment centre is Causeway Bay. Several department stores, including World Trade Centre, Fashion Walk, and SOGO, assemble the region. This developing area also offers a variety of Japanese supermarkets and boutiques for visitors. Take pleasure in shopping and travel to popular tourist destinations including Victoria Park and the Cross Harbour Tunnel.

TSUI TSIM SHA

Tsim Sha Tsui, another vibrant business district of Hong Kong, is home to boutique apparel and accessory shops and features distinctive buildings such as the Kowloon Mosque, Hong Kong Observatory, and the former headquarters of the Hong Kong Marine Police. In Tsim Sha Tsui, some of the most well-known shopping centres are Park Lane Shopper's Boulevard, Granville Square, Lok Road, and so on.

KHOEN KOK

On the Kowloon Peninsula, Mong Kok is a neighbourhood inside the Yau Tsim Mong District. Mong Kok, which translates to "the flourishing corner" in Cantonese, is home to a large number of retail stores, eateries, and entertainment options. The most famous street in Mong Kok is called Ladies' Street or Tung Choi Street, and it has a wide selection of accessories, makeup, and clothing. Other Mong Kok streets that tourists may find interesting are Sai Yeung Choi Street South, which is lined with stores offering cheap books, cosmetics, and consumer electronics; Temple Street (also known as Men's Street), which is well-known for its locally made goods from Hong Kong; Fa Yuen Street, which is lined with small shops selling apparel and sports gear; Portland Street, which is also known as the red light district in Hong Kong; and numerous other streets like Bird Garden, Flower Market Road, Goldfish Market, Tile Street, and Photocopy Street.

TOURS OF AMUSEMENT PARKS

HONG KONG AMUSEMENT PARK

The 40 hectare Hong Kong Disneyland is located on Lantau Island and opened for business in September 2005. This fantastical theme park is a popular destination for tourists of all ages and offers multilingual Mandarin, English, and Cantonese services. No matter your age or nationality, go to Hong Kong Disneyland and have an amazing time!
Location: Island of Lantau

HONG KONG'S OCEAN PARK

Located at Wong Chuk Hang and Nam Long Shan in the Southern District of Hong Kong, Ocean Park Hong Kong is a marine-themed theme park. Ocean Park Hong Kong, which opened its doors in 1997, is widely recognised as the seventh most popular amusement park worldwide. An An and Jia Jia, two cute giant pandas, and the largest aquarium in the world are among the many recreational amenities available at Ocean Park Hong Kong.
Place: Island of Hong Kong

NIGHT TOURS

VICTORIA PEAK, THE PEAK

The 552-meter-tall Victoria Peak (also known as Mount Austin) is a mountain on Hong Kong Island's western region. One of the top four places in the world to see breathtaking nighttime views of Victoria Harbour, the surrounding islands, and central Hong Kong is The Peak. To enjoy breathtaking views and visit the famed Madame Tussaud's Wax Museum of Hong Kong, visitors can ride the peak tram.

HARBOUR VICTORIA

Victoria Harbour, which is located between Kowloon Peninsula and Hong Kong Island, is one of the city's most popular tourist destinations and offers breathtaking scenery. As you take in the breathtaking views of the harbour, you won't want to miss seeing the Avenue of Stars, another popular tourist destination in Victoria Harbour.

PARK AT HONG KONG OCEAN

Located near the southernmost point of Hong Kong Island, Ocean Park Hong Kong is a globally renowned theme park. This well-known theme park also promotes environmental preservation and education. It is 880.000 square metres in size. The non-profit "Ocean Park Corporation" oversees this park, and its mission is to provide inexpensive recreation for all Hong Kong residents. Over four million people visit Ocean Park Hong Kong annually. Thirty thousand schoolchildren from Hong Kong are among them; they enjoy a happy excursion to the park and learn about animals. People in Hong Kong adore this park because it offers enjoyable and insightful guided programmes. With over 30 years of experience as a top tourist destination in Hong Kong, Ocean Park Hong Kong attracts guests from all over the world who come to take advantage of its amenities. The park provides guests with information, education, and conservation programmes in addition to exciting rides and a diverse range of performances. The Headland and Lowland are the two areas that make up Ocean Park Hong Kong. A variety of thrilling and exciting attractions, such as the Dragon, Eagle, Mine Train, Abyss Turbo Drop, Crazy Galleon, Flying Swing, Raging River, Ferris Wheel, Ocean Park Tower, and Space Wheel, are available to tourists in Headland. Everyone is in for an incredibly entertaining and exciting time. Visitors to Lowland get the opportunity to ride on the balloon that will ascend 100 metres into the sky as part of SkyFair. Giant pandas can also be seen in lowland areas by visitors. The finest places for families to visit include other attractions like Amazing Amazon, Amazing Birds Theatre, and Kid's World. In particular, Dolphin University at Kid's World allows guests to get up close and personal with dolphins while learning more about these amazing animals. The Terrace Cafe and The Bayview Restaurant, two recently completed buildings with an amazing sea view, welcome guests with a calm and seaside atmosphere.

The largest Taoist temple in Hong Kong is Yuen Wong Tai Sin Temple of Sik Sik Wong Tai Sin Temple. About 18,000 m2 make up the entire region. It is the most well-known and visited temple, and it honours the everlasting Wong Tai Sin. The temple, located north of Kowloon on the southern side of Lion Rock, is well-known for the Wong spiritual and "the fortune tellers."

It is well known that from Qiaoshan, Guangxi, China to Wan Chai, Hong Kong, a man by the name of Leung Renyan narrated the tale of Wong Tai Sin. A portrait of a man, depicting Wong Tai Sin himself when he was first transported to Hong Kong from

Guangdong in 1915, was placed on the centre altar. A distinguished individual proposed a better site in 1921; nonetheless, the temple was moved to Rosy Garden until the present.

Due to its historical value, the Temple has been designated as a Grade II historic building.

The daily hours of Wong Tai Sin Temple are 7 a.m. to 6 p.m. Tuesdays through Sundays from 9 a.m. to 4 p.m. when the garden is open. Donations are very appreciated, but there is no charge for either.

KUNG SAI

In the Hong Kong Special Administrative Region, to the south of the Saigon Peninsula and adjacent to the Saigon Sea, is the city known as Saigon. Since the fourteenth century, Saigon has been a fishing city. Furthermore, Saigon's name dates back to China's Ming Dynasty, when the city served as a port for other nations to pay tribute to China. Saigon is now the greatest place to sample fresh seafood if you're looking for one. Saigon Port's streets are lined with numerous seafood-themed stores and eateries.

The bus is Saigon's primary means of transportation between villages. The primary Hong Kong Railway transition station for travelling from downtown to Saigon is Rainbow Station. Additionally, you can rent a boat from a public pier and take in the Saigon Sea's island landscape. Saigon's distinct appeal is beckoning you to explore its basic yet enchanting isle aura.

CENTRAL

Central is the administrative and business centre of Hong Kong; it is situated across Victoria Harbour from Tsim Sha Tsui. This neighbourhood is home to numerous amazing skyscrapers; the AIG Tower and International Finance Centre are just two examples of the many big structures in the area. In order to establish connections with other Asian nations, the majority of multinational financial services organisations and worldwide international businesses have their headquarters in this region.

Additionally, the government headquarters are located on Government Hill, which is located in Central. You won't miss some of Central's well-known avenues and locations to learn about a lot of fascinating topics. Travellers can ride the peak tram to reach Victoria Peak, where they can purchase mementos and enjoy a breathtaking view of Hong Kong. If you enjoy shopping, you should definitely take a stroll down Pedder Street, where several well-known brand-name retailers showcase the newest merchandise. In Central, there's no shortage of eateries offering a diverse range of dishes to suit your palate. The finest area for those who enjoy going to pubs and clubs is Lan Kwai Fong, which has a large number of these establishments. Lan Kwai Fong is a popular hangout for young people and artists, where you may enjoy a glass of champagne with your pals at night.

BAY CAUSEWAY

For residents in particular, Causeway Bay, Hong Kong, is perhaps the most well-liked shopping destination on the island. It's situated in the island of Hong Kong's center. Admiralty has just two MTR stations. One of the primary MTR stations connecting Hong Kong and Kowloon. In order to accommodate the crowds on weekends, some side streets are actually quite near to the main road. The center of Causeway Bay is located just across Yee

Woo Street and is encircled by a wide variety of stores, eateries, hairdressers, movie theaters, and hotels of all kinds. The most well-known park in Hong Kong, Victoria Park, is positioned between Tin Hau and Causeway Bay. A marina/typhoon shelter is located on the waterfront. Due to the scarcity of reasonably priced real estate on the street level, the majority of restaurants have relocated upstairs. Time Square, Hennessy Centre, Island Beverly, Lee Theatre Plaza, and Time Square are a few buildings that have eateries on stories above ground. Almost all forms of transportation, including buses, min-buses, trams, MTR and taxis, can get you to Causeway Bay. The MTR is the most affordable and convenient. The blue line represents the MTR. Simply exit at the stop and proceed to your destination by following the signage within the station.

HONG KONG HISTORICAL MUSEUM
In addition to being a history museum, Hong Kong Museum of History is home to numerous art collections. The museum, which is next to the Hong Kong Science Museum in Tsim Sha Tsui, was founded in July 1975. Hong Kong's historical and cultural legacy is conserved by the Hong Kong

Museum of History. The museum typically hosts a number of exhibitions to introduce the evolution of Hong Kong as a world-class city and events capital, with the goal of educating visitors about the history of Hong Kong. You'll observe that the museum's holdings cover local history, archaeology, natural history, and ethnography. You can view some of the special and permanent exhibitions at the Hong Kong Museum of History to gain additional insight into the city. The narrative of the permanent exhibition begins 400 million years ago, during the Devonian period, and ends in 1997 with Hong Kong's reunification with China. Heavenly Horse, the most recent special exhibition, features Chinese art and culture through the horse. Just take in the displays at the Hong Kong Museum of History. These displays provide everyone with a clear understanding of Hong Kong's natural environment, folk culture, and historical progress while also being fun and informative.

TEMPLE MAN MO

Man Mo Temple, the early Chinese functional centre, was erected in 1847 in honour of two Chinese gods: Man Cheong, Man Tai, the deity of literature, and Mo Tai, Kwan Yu, the god of war. It's situated in the northwest of Hong Kong Island on

Hollywood Road in the Sheung Wan neighbourhood. Man Mo Temple, which has been overseen by the largest and oldest charity organisation, Tung Wah Group of Hospitals, since 1908, is a significant national monument and a well-known traditional Chinese temple for all Hong Kong residents. Every 8am the temple opens until 6 p.m. Man Mo Temple's golden altar is where you will find both Man Cheong and Mo Tai. Man Tai, in command of military and warfare, is seen holding a long, straight sword and a green robe, while Man Cheong, holding a brush, represents him as in charge of literature and the arts. Within Man Mo Temple are not only Man Cheong and Mo Tai, but also God Bao Zheng and Town God. Town God safeguards the community and symbolises livelihood, whereas God Bao Zheng stands for justice. In passing, you will notice a palanquin, a big bell, and a coppery incense burner close to the gate; these historical artifacts symbolize Hong Kong's lengthy past.

THE PEAK, VICTORIA PEAK
One of the most well-known tourist destinations is Victoria Peak, commonly known as Mount Austin, which is situated in the middle of the Hong Kong

Special Administrative Region. The peak of Victoria Peak, which is thought to be 552 metres high, is known to the locals as "The Peak." The neighbourhood around The Peak Station, home of The Peak Gondola, is referred known as "The Peak area." More specifically, Qi Li Mount, Ge Fu Mount, Kwun Lung Jiao, and Victoria Peak are all part of The Peak. The residence of the opulent houses held by the wealthy tycoons and international delegates is another highlight. The region beneath Victoria Peak is divided into Sheung Wan and Central, the latter of which became the primary business district.

Many expats have chosen to make The Peak their home in Hong Kong because of the breathtaking view and pleasant weather. The Peak Gondola opened for business in 1888, and the dramatic fire there took place in 1938. Even without renovation, The Peak Gondola continued to serve as the bus terminal station. The Peak Plaza rose to prominence as one of the most well-known tourist destinations until 1990.

You might not want to miss The Peak's breathtaking beauty when visiting Victoria Peak. The views of Victoria Harbour and Central may be pleasing to you. Additionally, you could enjoy shopping at The Peak Gondola's terminal station,

Ling Xiao Ge. You might find the ornate handicrafts and souvenirs within. Madame Tussauds Hong Kong is likewise situated in Ling Xiao Ge; you may enjoy the colourful wax sculptures for a happy trip to Hong Kong.

STREET TEMPLE

Named after a temple dedicated to Tin Hau, Temple Street was constructed during the Qing Dynasty. The area is referred to as Men's Street at times. Compare that to Mong Kok's Tung Choi Street Ladies' Market. Temple Street is situated in Kowloon, Hong Kong, between the Jordan and Yau Ma Tei neighbourhoods. It is widely renowned for its Night Market, which is a great spot to eat a hearty lunch and find some great deals. Locals and visitors alike enjoy coming here in the evening to purchase inexpensive goods and food items. Visiting Yau Ma Tei's Temple Street is simple. It's just a short walk to the left once you take the Nathan Road MTR exit. Going here after 7:00 p.m. is the ideal option if you want to have a fascinating experience with the bustling night market during its busiest times of day. Every night, Temple Street hosts little concerts. On their own area of the street, you may see groups of Cantonese opera singers performing classic tunes. Furthermore, this location serves as a treasure island for collectors. This region of Hong Kong offers reasonably priced antiques, high-end audio equipment, and vintage CD collections.

AIRPORT INTERNATIONAL IN HONG KONG

In addition to being a major tourist destination in Hong Kong, Hong Kong International Airport (HKIA) has made a name for itself as a major driver of economic growth for both the PRD region and Hong Kong. In addition to being a top-notch airport, HKIA is notable for its core services, amenities, and passenger experience. In order to provide travellers a pleasurable and distinctive airport experience, HKIA's two terminals, Terminals 1 and 2, are furnished with a range of boutiques, restaurants, leisure areas, and telecommunication services. Specifically, SkyPlaza in T2 and SkyMart in T1 provide diners and shoppers an enjoyable and comfortable airport experience. With an eye towards the future, HKIA is evolving into an airport city from just an airport serving a metropolis. Apart from T2, noteworthy projects include the Hong Kong SkyCity Marriott Hotel and the SkyCity Nine Eagles Golf Course, which is a second airport hotel.

The other project was scheduled to debut in late 2008, while the golf course already had its grand opening in 2007 back then. According to the annual Skytrax study, HKIA has been named the finest airport in the world six times in the last seven years. Passengers may even enjoy spending time at the airport watching planes take off and land on the runway.

HONG KONG INTERNATIONAL THEME PARKS, an incorporated business that is jointly owned by The Walt Disney Company and the Government of Hong Kong, is responsible for the ownership and management of Hong Kong Disneyland. On September 12, 2005, Hong Kong Disneyland, the fifth Disneyland-style park, officially opened to the public. The park is divided into three themed areas called Fantasyland, Adventureland, and Tomorrowland that are reminiscent of earlier Disneyland park initiatives. On April 28, 2008, the beloved Disney theme, It's A Small World, will open. In addition, Hong Kong

Disneyland's managing director and executive vice president, Bill Ernest, announced that the park intends to build two more theme areas in the future. At that point, the occupied land will total little more than 100 acres. The employees of the theme park are bilingual in Chinese and English. Chinese, Japanese, and English versions of the guide maps are printed to make sure that everyone has a fantastic day.

VICTORIA HARBOUR

The harbour that separates Hong Kong, China's Hong Kong Island from the Kowloon Peninsula is called Victoria Harbour. About 42 km2 are covered by its sheltering area and natural depth.

A famous nighttime skyline and view of Victoria Harbour are breathtakingly beautiful. Victoria Harbour is especially located with the skyline above the sky behind it, facing Hong Kong Island. The piazza at the Culture Centre and the Victoria Tower atop Victoria Peak are two of the greatest spots to see the harbour. Another favourite activity is taking a ride on the Star Ferry to see the waterfront.

Numerous significant public events, such as the yearly fireworks display on the second night of the Lunar New Year, have taken place at the waterfront. The government added a display that featured a symphony of lights, music, lights, and pyrotechnics to promote Hong Kong to its viewers every evening in addition to the harbor's prominence as a sightseeing destination.

STREET OF STARS

One of the most well-liked attractions in Hong Kong is The Avenue of Stars!

The Avenue of Stars, a 440-meter promenade that honours the stars of the Hong Kong film industry while elevating tourism in the city, is situated along the waterfront of the stunning Victoria Harbour around the New World Centre in Tsim Sha Tsui East, Kowloon. The New World Group is the sponsor of the HKD 40 million Avenue of Stars promenade project, which is also supported by the Hong Kong Film Awards Association Limited, the Leisure and Cultural Services Department, the Tourism Commission, and the Hong Kong Tourism Board. The Avenue of Stars in Hollywood served as the model for the architecture.

Visitors can choose to visit the Avenue of Stars at any time of day or night because it is a free attraction. The promenade's abundance of dazzling lights beside the buildings creates a breathtaking nighttime view. Another must-see attraction of this popular Hong Kong site is the Symphony of Lights, which is performed here at night.

Along with breathtaking nighttime views, the Avenue of Stars features a video chronicling the history of the local film industry and over 100 plaques bearing the handprints of well-known actors and actresses from Hong Kong. The 3-meter-tall bronze monument of renowned kung fu star Bruce Lee is the most photographed location along the Avenue of Stars. In addition to posing for photos with the Bruce Lee and celebrity plaques, you may explore and find the Oscar statue as well as numerous other sculptures relating to movies. Snack shops and souvenir shops are a great place to relax while admiring the picturesque views of Victoria Harbour.

Lan Kwai Fong, often known as SoHo, is a pedestrian-only square in Central, Hong Kong. It encompasses D'Aguilar Street, Wellington Street, and Wyndham Street broadly and is currently a well-liked destination for dining, drinking, and partying in Hong Kong.

The Lan Kwai Fong used to be a street filled of Mui Yan (middle people), or women who worked as marriage agencies, many years ago. Mui Yan acts as a middleman in marriages between two households. As a result, Mui Yan Hong and Hong Leung Hong (middle person lane) became well-known by this name. Allan Zeman, the father of Lan Kwai Fong, spent 32 million Hong Kong dollars in the 1980s to purchase a large building and decorate it with Western-style dining establishments. The location quickly developed into a gathering spot for immigrants in Hong Kong. A homosexual disco called "Disco Disco" was established on D'Aguilar Street in the interim. These two prosperous ventures turned Lan Kwai Fong and the surrounding area into a well-known destination for nightlife. This is a spot that you simply MUST visit at night. For the newest and hottest nightlife in the city, head over to Lan Kwai Fong. Spend time dancing or enjoying a wide variety of beverages at the bar while hanging out with friends in one of the hip clubs. At your favourite sports bar, you may also cheer for your team. It's possible that the waiter or waitress knows your name if you return to any bar.

KONG'S MADAME TUSSAUDS

One of the attractions you really shouldn't miss when visiting the Victoria Peak is Madame Tussauds Hong Kong, along with the breathtaking views that overlook Kowloon Peninsula and Hong Kong Island. At the Madame Tussauds Hong Kong wax museum, you can see lifelike replicas of local and global personalities.

In the year 2000, the Madame Tussauds Wax Museum of Hong Kong held its grand opening. Madame Tussauds's origins can be found in the year 1770. At the Palace of Versailles in France, Madame Tussaud tutored the sister of King Louis XVI in art after learning the craft from Dr. Philippe Curtius. Madame Tussauds was compelled to create death masks of the executed aristocracy during the French Revolution as a sign of her loyalty to the feudalistic nobles. Early in the 19th century, she set out for Britain and conducted a number of exhibitions featuring revolutionary artefacts and effigies of popular villains and heroes.

As time went on, Madame Tussauds' exhibits began to resemble mobile newspapers, offering the public access to the people who made headlines and insights into world events. Madame Tussauds opened her first permanent exhibition space on Baker Street in London in 1835. In 1884, the company moved to its current location on Marylebone Road. The guillotine that was used to behead Marie Antoinette and the death masks Madame Tussauds was ordered to manufacture during the French Revolution are among the original and early works and artefacts that are still on display in London.

The first Madame Tussauds location in Asia is in Hong Kong. Regularly added are new figures that depict popular global events. Its first expansion took place from September 2005 to May 2006. Hollywood Stars, Asian Stars, Cultural Figures, Sports Stars, Pop Stars, Royalty Members, World Leaders, Fashion Icons, and Kung Fu Stars are among the nine categories offered by this Hong Kong branch. The wax figures that are currently on display include the following list.

Jackie Chan, Bruce Lee, and Michelle Yeoh are Kung Fu Stars; Elle Macpherson and Naomi Campbell are Fashion Icons.

World Leaders: Lee Kwan Yew, Diana, Queen Elizabeth II, Hu Jintao, Deng Xiao Ping, Mao Zedong, Mahatma Gandhi, Wen Jiabao, Donald Tsang, Barack Obama, Hu Jintao, and Wen Jiabao The Duke of Edir Pop Stars: Madonna, Miriam Yeung, Joey Yung, Michael Jackson, Teresa Teng, Anita Mui, Elvis Presley, and the Beatles

SPORTS STARS: Muhammad Ali, David Beckham, Ronaldinho, Liu Xiang, Yao Ming, and Lee Lai Shan

CULTURAL ICONS: Mozard, Luciano Pavarotti, Rembrandt van Rijn, Madam Tussauds, and Pablo Picasso

HOLLYWOOD STARS: Sir Anthony Hopkins, Jodie Foster, Marilyn Monroe, Brad Pitt, Johnny Depp, Harrison Ford, and Angelina Jolie

ASIAN SUPERSTARS: Andy Lau, Leon Lai, Connie Chan, Cecilia Cheung, Kelly Chen, Barbie Hsu, Louis Koo, Aaron Kwok, Bae Yong Joon, Leslie Cheung, and Andy Lau

Have you ever had fantasies of posing for photos with your favourite celebrities and stars? Visit Madame Tussauds Hong Kong to view the remarkably accurate wax replicas of the people you hold dear! Hold their hands and snap photos while saying "Say cheese"! Please visit http://www.madametussauds.com/hongkong/ for additional information about Madame Tussauds Hong Kong...

opening times
Hours of Operation: 10:00 - 22:00. Entry-level: 21:45

spending synopsis:
1. The cost of the 2-in-1 combo package (admission ticket + peak tram)

In both directions:
Adult: HKD 180; Child: HKD 90 (three to eleven years old)
Senior: HKD 90 (65 years of age or older)

One Method:

Adult: HKD 170; Child: HKD 85 (three to eleven years old)

Senior: HKD 85 (65 years of age or older)

2. The 3-in-1 Combo Package (Admission Ticket + Sky Terrace + Peak Tram)

Returning to Madame Tussauds and Sky Terrace by Peak Tram

Adult: $200 HKD

Youngster (ages 3 to 11): HKD 100

Senior: HKD 100 (65 years of age or older)

Sky Terrace + Madame Tussauds + Single Peak Tram

Adult: HKD 190; Child (three to eleven years old): HKD 95

Senior: HKD 95 (65 years of age or older)

Note: Garden Road Peak Tram Terminus offers the combo package (sales counter open 9:30–21:30).

Chapter 8

THE WORLD OF FROZEN AT DISNEYLAND IN HONG KONG

We simply cannot accept that Hong Kong Disneyland's World of Frozen will open so soon! We're here to provide you all the information you need to know before visiting this Frozen-themed land when it opens on November. We have all the information you need to plan your trip to World of Frozen, from two brand-new attractions to brand-new cuisine.

There are two areas in World of Frozen: Arendelle Forest and Arendelle Village.

The majority of the population resides in the village, which is also home to Northern Delights, Tick Tock Toys & Collectibles, Golden Crocus Inn, and Frozen Ever After.

In addition, it is the location of other well-known sites, including the North Mountain with Elsa's Ice Palace, Arendelle Castle, Friendship Fountain, and Clock Tower Square. The settlement is connected to the forest side by King Agnarr Bridge, which bears the name of the father of Anna and Elsa and the former king of Arendelle. On the forest side are Wandering Oaken's Sliding Sleighs, Playhouse in the Woods, Forest Fare, and Travelling Traders.

Which rides are available at World Frozen?
Oaken's Sliding Sleighs on the Run
Hong Kong Disneyland's family-friendly coaster, Wandering Oaken's Sliding Sleighs, was constructed just in time for Summer Snow Day! You will pass through the quaint Trading Post, which has a variety of winter wonders and pleasant summer goods on display, before boarding. Of course, Oaken is also here, waiting to welcome you from his sauna, his face obscured by the mist that falls from the window.

Travelling to the loading area, you can hop into a sleigh that is adorned with motifs that echo Kristoff's sleigh. You will climb to the top with Olaf and Kristoff's reindeer, Sven, and go on a thrilling adventure through the forest with breathtaking vistas of the surrounding area.

A Happy Ever After
There's a magical boat excursion in Frozen Ever After that the whole family will love! You will go

through the North Mountain to witness Troll Valley, Elsa's Ice Palace, and other sights.

Throughout, you'll run into your beloved characters, Olaf and Sven, who ask you if you'd like to build a snowman when you first set out on your journey. At Hong Kong Disneyland, these characters have never come to life thanks to the most cutting-edge Audio-Animatronics figures ever created.

Where can I get food in Frozen World?

Vibrant Crocus Hotel
Do you need a filling meal? Your destination is Golden Crocus Inn! From seafood to pasta, this quaint, nautically styled quick service restaurant in Arendelle Village offers a wide range of delectable dishes inspired by hearty, Norwegian fare.

Sights in the North
What is that lovely scent? Naturally, chocolate! This classic confection is available at Northern Delights in Arendelle Village and is a must-try at World of Frozen. This posh neighbourhood candy store offers an extensive selection of packaged gift confectionary, baked products, and desserts.

Forest Dinner
If you feel like having a snack after a long day of exploring, Forest Fare has you covered! This charming cart offers shaved ice, pastries, churros, and more at Arendelle Forest. It's all you need to take on Arendelle—a little extra gasoline.

Where are Oaken, Kristoff, Anna, and Elsa going to be?

Gazebo in the Forest
Playhouse in the Woods, Elsa's hidden childhood retreat, is now open! Using singing, projection mapping, special effects, and sensory elements, Anna, Elsa, and Olaf come to life in this first-of-its-kind, distinctive, and captivating theatrical experience located in Arendelle Forest.

Character Interactions
There are additional Frozen buddies spread out across the country in addition to meeting Anna and Elsa at Playhouse in the Woods. Ask Kristoff for his best ice tips or say "hoo hoo" to Oaken; they can't wait to celebrate Summer Snow Day with you!

Where can I get items related to World of Frozen?

Tick-Tock Collectibles & Toys

Tick Tock Toys, a beloved and centuries-old toy store in Arendelle Village, has all the best souvenirs! Everything from cute headbands with an Olaf theme to jumpers with a Nordic flair, there is something for everyone. Additionally, don't forget to check out the "Royal Post of Arendelle," where you may mail postcards to loved ones, which is situated directly outside the store.

Itinerant Merchants

This Arendelle Forest pop-up store is the ideal place to get inexpensive gifts including headbands, shoulder stuffed animals, keychains, and more!

At World of Frozen, there are endless activities available, including Frozen brain freeze! Not yet persuaded? Here are six reasons to visit Hong Kong Disneyland as soon as the gates open on November 20.

Culinary Guide to the World of Frozen, Available November.

You're going to be confused by flavour, so hold on to your appetite. On November 20, Hong Kong Disneyland Resort will welcome World of Frozen, a brand-new area brimming with delectable foods and confections inspired by the adored characters of these critically acclaimed Walt Disney Animation Studios productions, "Frozen" and "Frozen 2." You will be greeted with stunning scenery, must-see sites, enthralling music, and an abundance of food as soon as you enter Arendelle!

When this exciting expansion opens, there will be three more sites that you can visit and enjoy delicious cuisine and sweet sweets. And you know that this kingdom inspired by "Frozen" has to have some chocolate.

Golden Crocus Inn, the brand-new quick-service restaurant, will be offering delicious main course selections, including a Celebration Chocolate Fondue. Yes, chocolate fondue—you read that right! Northern Delights is the place to go if you're looking for a delicious assortment of goods inspired by "Frozen." Beautiful nibbles, such as the Olaf Celebration Cake, abound on its menu. Trust me when I say that these dishes, which the culinary teams lovingly created, will melt anyone's heart! Last but not least, "Frozen"-inspired sweet and savoury dishes, such as the lovely Snowflake Churros, will be available at Forest Fare.

When it comes to cuisine, World of Frozen genuinely has something to offer everyone. And it's definitely worth melting for these treats. Starting on November 20, let's prepare to unlock the gates and see what lies ahead.

The Innkeeper's Special Braised Lamb Shank, the Village Chicken Roll Stuffed with Ham and Cheese, the Bayside Seafood Medley and the Forest Mushroom Pasta at Golden Crocus Inn

Accompanied by potatoes, cream sauce, and a brown sugar roll, the Bayside Seafood Medley
Village Pita Pizza stuffed with cheese and gammon and served with mustard cream sauce and sautéed veggies
The Innkeeper's Special Braised Lamb Shank comes with roasted veggies, beer gravy, and polenta potato purée.
Pasta with woodland mushrooms, a poached egg, and a truffle cream sauce is provided with the dish.
Meatballs and Pasta with Forest Mushrooms Platter with mushroom cream sauce and sautéed veggies (The kids' meal selection)

Arendelle Meatballs in Mushroom Cream Sauce, Prawn Cocktail, and Rosettes
Cocktail with Prawns (Side offering)
Meatballs with Arendelle in a Mushroom Cream Sauce (Side dish)
Rosettes (Compatible with every main course served)

- Chocolate Fondue for a Celebration Available with all main meal selections is the non-alcoholic chocolate fondue jasmine peach fanta.

- **Northern Delights**: Olaf Snowflake Smultringer, Olaf Celebration Cupcake, North Mountain Almond Tart, and Coronation Sundae

- **Coronation Sundae**: Soft serve sundae with light milk served on elderflower-flavored slush (served in a cup with a "Frozen" theme).

- White chocolate cream and bergamot combine in the North Mountain Almond Tart.

- **Olaf Celebration Cupcake**: Creamy frosting topped with carrot and dried fruit cake

- Olaf Smultringer - Snowflakes

- Olaf Muffin, Marshmallow Lollipop, Candy Apple Snowball, Northern Delights Chocolate Box, and Olaf Muffin

- **Olaf Muffin**: An Olaf-inspired blueberry muffin with cream icing DreamWorks Munchling

- Snow Day Soft-serve Summer

- The Chocolate Box from Northern Delights

- Snowball of Candy Apples

- Day of Summer Snow Marshmallows

- Candy Marshmallow Pop

- Olaf Candies

- Snowflake Churros, Cookies with Forest Valley Tea, Platter of Sausages, Gourmet Box of Forest Fare and Forest Friends Forest Fare at Stein

Frosty Churros
Tea Cookies and Sausage Platter from Forest Valley (available seasonally)
The Forest Fare Gourmet Box includes items such as corn salad and crab sticks, cheese and tomato sauce on chicken buns, and blueberry and coconut cheese cream over crepes.

Mango-flavored shaved ice was provided beside the Forest Friends Stein.
Whether you share my excitement or not, I can't wait for this exciting new opening on November 20! As you can see, there are countless adventures to be had in Disney Parks, particularly when it comes to cuisine.

SPECIAL OCCASIONS

Year Of The Chinese

Participate in the exciting celebrations of Chinese New Year in January and February. The park is filled with vibrant lanterns and red envelopes as you feel the rhythm of the drums and gongs and marvel at the spirited lion dances. Savour the unique Chinese holiday cuisine that the park has to offer. Tickets with specified dates are sold for attendance during this busy time.

- Christmas From mid-November to the end of December, HK Disneyland welcomes Christmas. Christmas trees, carolers, baubles, bows, fluffy snow, and more are all there, along with Christmas parades. Make sure to stay until the sun sets to witness the spectacular display of Christmas lights.

- October 31st: HK Disneyland celebrates Halloween in October with spectral parades, haunting trees, and creepy pumpkin patches. For trick-or-treaters courageous enough to brave the streets populated with Disney villains, there's also candy.

LEADING ATTRACTIONS
- Large Runaway Mine Cars in Grizzly Mountains

- Take a rollercoaster ride through a steep canyon, past blasting dynamite and rearing grizzly bears, and into a darkened mine tunnel. As soon as you believe you are clear, you are launched into a new shaft and hurtle past frolicking fountains and sheer canyon walls.

- **Space Needle**: Here in Hong Kong is the renownedly exhilarating rollercoaster with a space theme that operates at night. Bold cosmonauts can launch themselves into space on a rocket, hurtling past satellites and meteors before feeling gravity's pull as they reenter the atmosphere.

- **Magical Manor**: Popular with guests of all ages, the hilariously haunted mansion experience showcases Disney's mastery of visual effects. Navigate eight galleries to witness the eruption of Mount Vesuvius, avoid a plant that devours humans, and meet the fabled Monkey King.

- **RC Vehicle**: As you board the 20-person vehicle and are practically upside down on a 27-meter U-shaped racecourse, the highest point in Toy Story Land, get ready for huge dips and thrills.

- **Animation School**: In the Animation Academy outside the entrance, discover the techniques of the cartoon trade and take a class with a real Disney artist to learn how to draw a Disney character. Please take note that these programmes are only available in Cantonese.

- **That Small World**: This beloved Disney classic is enjoyed by all. Sail around on a small boat with a cast of about three hundred papier-mâché kids dressed in regional costumes, singing the well-known tune. The Hong Kong edition is unlike any other in the world thanks to special additions that showcase Chinese and Hong Kong history.

Chapter 9

SERVICE FOR DISABILITY ACCESS ("DAS")

DAS is intended for visitors with impairments who find it difficult to endure long waits in a traditional line setting. With the help of this service, visitors can plan a return time that is close to the current wait time in queue for the specified attractions. It doesn't provide you instant access to the attraction. If a visitor's impairment is limited to the need for a wheelchair or scooter, they can benefit from alternative accommodations offered by the Park without the need for DAS. Visitors using wheelchairs or scooters will either be required to wait in the regular queue or be given a return time at the attraction that is equivalent to the existing standby wait, depending on the attraction.

Please get in touch with visitor Relations if you have any queries or concerns about mobility as a visitor.

The following Hong Kong Disneyland Park authorized attractions accept DAS:

- Animation School

- Ant-Man vs. Wasp: Nano Conflict!

- Large Runaway Mine Cars in Grizzly Mountains

- A Cinderella Story Turntable

- The Lion King Festival featuring Dumbo the Flying Elephant

- Hong Regime Hyperspace Railroad at Disneyland Elevation

- Experience Iron Man – Presented by AIA

- "A small world, that is"

- A Jungle River Tour

- Cups of Mad Hatters Tea

- The Multiverse Explorations of Winnie the Pooh

- Mickey and the Amazing Novel

- Mickey's Magical Mystic Manor Phlihar

- Orbitron RC Racers to Tarzan's Treehouse

- Toy Soldier Spin Toy Slinky Dog Parachute Drop

- Only the day of registration is DAS valid.

METHODS FOR APPLYING FOR A DAS CARD

In order to register and receive the DAS card, a guest wishing to use DAS must come in person to City Hall and show our cast members the appropriate, valid form of identification or documentation (such as the Registration Card for People with Disabilities issued by the Government of Hong Kong Special Administrative Region).

- The DAS card cover will display the name, party size, and valid date of each registered visitor, along with any pertinent identification or document number.

UTILIZING THE DAS CARD

- A maximum of five additional guests who are also registered users of DAS may do so (together, the "DAS party").

- The registered passenger must show the DAS card to the admission greeter at the selected attraction in order to obtain a DAS return time.

- The greeter will show a DAS return time on the DAS card if the advertised wait time is fifteen (15) minutes longer.

- The registered visitor and the DAS party will be directed to the proper queue if the posted wait time is less than or equal to fifteen (15) minutes.

- When it's time to leave the attraction, the registered guest and the DAS party must personally show the DAS card to the entrance greeter in order to use the DAS return time. The DAS party and the registered visitor will go straight to the proper queue. The DAS card will have the greeter indicate "completed" next to the DAS return time.

- In the event of a theatre performance, the registered visitor may, subject to seat availability, request a DAS return time for a designated show session at the theater's entrance at least one hour prior to the designated show session's start time. When the DAS returns, the registered visitor and the DAS party must physically show the DAS card to the entrance greeter and heed the cast members' directions to enter the theatre. The DAS return time will be lost if the designated show session has begun and neither the registered visitor nor the DAS party have turned up. For a subsequent show session, the registered visitor must submit a fresh request for a new DAS return time.

- When redeeming a DAS return time, HKITP retains the right to ask the registered visitor to provide the necessary identification or documentation for verification.

- After visiting an attraction, the registered guest and the DAS party can use their DAS card to get a DAS return time at another approved attraction.

THE EASE OF ACCESS TO ATTRACTIONS

All of the attractions at Hong Kong Disneyland Park are accessible to visitors in wheelchairs.

At the park, different attraction needs transfer from a wheelchair to a ride system in order to access the following attractions:

- The Flying Elephant, Dumbo

- Cups of Mad Hatters Tea

- Hyperspace Mountain Orbitron

- Experience of Iron Man

- Toy Soldier RC Racer with Parachute Drop

- Grizzly Slinky Dog Spin Elevation Autonomous Mine Cars

- Main Road Automobiles

  ★ Ensemble Wheelchair users may not be physically transferred from their wheelchairs by Members. It is advisable for guests requiring assistance to travel with a helping companion.

Attractions That Don't Need a Transfer
Wheelchair users can board and ride at the following attractions while still seated:

- Cinderella Fantasy Gardens Carousel

- Disneyland Railway in Hong Kong

- "A small world, that is"

- River Cruises through the Jungle to Tarzan's Treehouse

- The Multiverse Explorations of Winnie the Pooh

- Mickey's PhilharMagic Mystic Manor Lion King Festival

- Animation Art

- A Fun-Filling Garden of Wonders

- Geyser Gulch Animation Academy / Lik Tikis

- Ant-Man vs. Wasp: Nano Conflict!

- Presented by Pandora, Mickey and the Wonderful Book Fairy Tale Forest

- Moana: A Celebration of Coming Home

HEARING DISABILITIES

INDUCTIVE LOOPS

Some attractions and services use inductive loop sound enhancement to help customers who need hearing aids communicate.

Available in:

- The Lion King Festival*

- Disney Storybook Theatre

- Mickey's Philharmagic

- The ticket box

- Customer service window

- Public transport

DIETARY REQUIREMENTS

All Hong Kong Disneyland Resort full service restaurants can accommodate most dietary requirements with advance notice.
Guests are encouraged to contact their chosen restaurant to make special arrangements or visit the Customer Contact Center for additional information and assistance.
entry

Almost all attractions, shops, restaurants and shows are open to all guests.
However, in some cases, customers may require assistance from other team members to fully utilize these areas.
Some attractions may require guests who use wheelchairs to transfer from their wheelchair to a wheelchair accessible system.

Cast members are not suited to physically transport guests in wheelchairs.

Therefore, it is recommended that you visit a person who can provide you with physical assistance if necessary.

Rules and Regulations for the Park for Visitors

Greetings from Disneyland Park in Hong Kong! They put a lot of effort into making sure every guest has a relaxing, secure, and joyful stay. By bearing the following in mind, you can assist them:

- Before entering the park and while within, screening and security checks may be conducted on all people, baggage, packages, clothing, and other objects.

- They reserve the right to prohibit the carrying of any bag, package, or other thing into the Park and to take necessary action against any items left unattended.

- Throughout their visit to the park, guests should keep their entry passes, tickets, and Magic Access membership cards. When asked by a cast member, they should provide these documents for verification.

- Outside food and drink products may be brought into the Park by visitors for their own use, so long as they don't need to be heated, reheated, processed, refrigerated, or temperature-controlled, and they don't smell strongly. Foods that are prohibited from being consumed in the Park include, but are not limited to, durian fruit, hot water-requiring quick noodles, and meals stored in containers that may be reheated.

- Please refrain from using foul language and from acting in a dangerous, unlawful, disruptive, or unpleasant manner towards other park visitors and our cast members as a courtesy. Please don't run for your safety or the safety of others.

- When parking and/or securing your pram, kindly heed the directions of Cast Members, abide by all signs and keep other Guests' safety in mind.

- Before departing from a store or retail outlet, please pay for any merchandise goods you have chosen at the payment counter there.

- During your visit, please be mindful of other park visitors and take care not to bump into, push or go ahead of them in the queue. The group as a whole needs to wait together as well. It is not permitted for party members to join those who are already in queue.

- At all times, appropriate clothing is required, including shoes and shirts. Costumes are not permitted for guests 16 years of age or older, unless we specifically allow or encourage it for special events or programmes. Anyone wearing clothing that we deem unsuitable or that would lessen the experience of other Guests may be refused entry or have their presence removed.

- Tobacco, e-cigarettes, and other items that emit smoke or vapor may only be smoked in specified places for the comfort of all visitors. Kindly get assistance from a cast member.

- You are always in charge of ensuring the safety and security of your personal property. Regardless of whether our fault or another factor led to the damage or loss, we disclaim all liability and are not accountable for any damage to a guest's property or belongings.

- At all times, please watch over your kids and take care of the elderly. To access the Park, guests under the age of sixteen must be escorted by a guest who is sixteen or older. Children under the age of seven must be accompanied by an adult who is at least 16 in order to board an attraction.

- The safety regulations specific to each attraction apply before entering.

- You must abide by all signs posted throughout the park and by Cast Members' instructions for the safety of other Park Visitors, Cast Members, and yourself.

- Before entering the Park, please show your ticket and allow us to take a picture of you, or provide any other legitimate form of identification that we may occasionally need for verification. Reentry into the Park requires the ticket, handstamp, photo, and/or any other applicable, valid form of personal identity. Before entering the park, please ask a cast member about other verification arrangements if you would prefer not to have your photo taken or the photo of your kids taken.

- The following terms and conditions apply: tickets, admittance media, Magic Access membership cards, and other benefits are revocable, non-transferable, non-exchangeable, and void if altered. Throughout its validity time, the ticket can only be used by one individual, and it is not good for special events that have an additional admission fee.

- It is forbidden to bring the following things into the park:

- Hazardous or dangerous substances. any type of weapon, as well as anything that could be mistaken for toy guns or other weapons.

- Alcoholic drinks or any prohibited drug.

- Glass containers—that is, excepting little ones like jars used for infant food.

- Any luggage, coolers, crates, or bags bigger than 56 x 36 x 23 cm. It is not allowed to put dry or loose ice in these containers. Ice packs that can be reused are advised.

- Any size of luggage on wheels. waggons, carts, or other wheeled carriers that aren't manual wheelchairs, electrically powered mobility aids that have three wheels or more and move at a walking speed, or strollers that aren't bigger than 92 by 132 cm.

- Animals (apart from assistance dogs). A guide dog or a dog trained to work or complete duties for and support a person with a disability is referred to as a service dog. At all times, service dogs must be kept under the owner's supervision and on a leash or harness. Certain attractions might not allow service dogs to ride them due to their nature.

- Guests sixteen years of age or older are not permitted to wear masks (unless necessary for medical reasons or legal compliance). Masks worn by younger guests must always include apertures that allow the wearer's eyes to be fully seen in their peripheral vision.

- Big tripods, stools, or foldable chairs.

- Wheeled recreational gadgets, such as skateboards, scooters, inline skates, and shoes with integrated wheels.

- Drones, kites, or other remotely controlled aircraft. Any size flags, banners, or signage.

- Other things that we think could be offensive, dangerous, or interfere with Park's or any related facility's ability to function/

- Items that are forbidden by any regulations in the People's Republic of China's Hong the usage of extension poles for cell phones or portable cameras (such as selfie sticks).

- Without their permission, the following activities are prohibited: selling or exchanging goods or services; offering goods or services for sale or exchange; soliciting offers to buy or sell goods or services; and selling or exchanging goods or services, with the exception of Disney-branded merchandise and tour and photography services of any kind. The dissemination of any type of printed or recorded material.

- Unauthorised public gatherings, including speeches, demonstrations, and the use of flags, banners, or signs to enrage crowds.

- Feeding all park animals, including birds.

- Tinkering with remote-controlled aircraft, drones, or kites.

- photography, filming, and recording of any kind—aside from for private use.

- Interacting with other visitors or interfering with the park's operations while pretending to be or portraying any fictional or real-life character, whether or not they are dressed in costume.

- participating in any risky behavior or other activity that could make it more difficult for the Park or any related facility to operate.

Chapter 10

CONCLUSION

The second largest Disneyland in Asia is located on Lantau Island in the heart of the Hong Kong Disneyland Resort.
Whether you're traveling as a couple, a group of adults, or a family with young children, be sure to visit Hong Kong Disneyland while you're in town.

It's a fun day out, and this huge theme park isn't far from central Hong Kong, so it's easy to get around.

There is a marine park nearby, but I recommend spending a day at Hong Kong Disneyland because there are so many fun things to explore.

Although it is one of the smallest Disney parks in the world, it is still very large and sprawling. Most visitors to the park come from mainland China, but tourists and residents from Hong Kong also frequent the park.

FAQS REGARDING DISNEYLAND IN HONG KONG

These are the most frequent questions from families that I assist with vacation planning to Hong Kong.

ARE THE PEOPLE AT DISNEYLAND HONG KONG ENGLISH SPEAKER?
Absolutely, the cast members speak Mandarin, Cantonese, and English. Reading guide maps, communicating with staff, and traversing the park will be a breeze for English speakers.

WHICH CASTLE IS SITUATED AT HONG KONG'S DISNEYLAND?

The Castle of Magical Dreams is the name of the castle at Hong Kong Disneyland. The only Disney castle devoted to all 14 Disney heroines and princesses is this one. This was the first time a Disney castle had ever been completely closed for renovations.

HOW FAR AWAY FROM THE AIRPORT IS DISNEYLAND HONG KONG?

The Hong Kong International Airport is located roughly 13 kilometers from the theme park. If there isn't any traffic, taking a taxi will take roughly fifteen minutes. Travel time by Airport Express train and MTR should be approximately thirty-five minutes.

HOW CAN I GO FROM THE AIRPORT TO DISNEYLAND HONG KONG?

Since Hong Kong Disneyland doesn't have an airport shuttle, the simplest way to get there is to take a blue Lantau taxi from the airport.

As an alternative, you can go to Tsing Yi station on the Airport Express train and change to the Tung Chung line there. To transfer to the Disneyland

Resort Line, take the Tung Chung line to Sunny Bay station.

CAN I AVOID BOOKING A HOTEL IN HONG KONG DISNEYLAND?

Staying at a hotel near Hong Kong Disneyland has many benefits. You'll get quick access to the park as well as extra benefits that are exclusive to hotel visitors. Unusual for Hong Kong, these hotels also accommodate families of four in two-bed rooms.

Still, a quick MTR trip from some of the world's top luxury hotels is possible in Hong Kong. Therefore, I suggest staying in Central or Kowloon if you enjoy staying in nice hotels.

WHICH MONTH IS BEST FOR VISITATION?

When it's not too hot and muggy, October through April is the ideal time of year to visit Hong Kong Disneyland. Because of the crowds, public holidays like Chinese New Year are best avoided when visiting. It's pleasant to go during the holidays because of the extra entertainment and joyful atmosphere.

ARE THERE MAGIC HOURS ADVANCED?

No, there aren't any Extra Magic Hours in Hong Kong Disneyland.

OCEAN PARK OR DISNEYLAND: SHOULD I GO?

Families discover that they can only visit one theme park in Hong Kong due to the abundance of things to do there. It's challenging to choose between Disneyland and Ocean Park, but there are a few things to think about. You will adore HKDL if you are a Disney enthusiast, do not currently live near a Disney park, or do not have any future plans to visit one.

Little ones have lots to do at Ocean Park, but teens prefer the roller coasters and other thrills. This is the spot to bring children who are interested in animals or marine life. It's interesting to visit a well-managed, secure, and relatively new theme park outside of your country of origin.